Lujo Brentano, William Arnold

Hours and wages in relation to production

Lujo Brentano, William Arnold

Hours and wages in relation to production

ISBN/EAN: 9783743312142

Hergestellt in Europa, USA, Kanada, Australien, Japan

Cover: Foto ©Suzi / pixelio.de

Manufactured and distributed by brebook publishing software
(www.brebook.com)

Lujo Brentano, William Arnold

Hours and wages in relation to production

HOURS AND WAGES

IN RELATION TO PRODUCTION

BY

LUJO BRENTANO

TRANSLATED BY MRS. WILLIAM ARNOLD

London

SWAN SONNENSCHEIN & CO.

NEW YORK: CHARLES SCRIBNER'S SONS

1894

BUTLER & TANNER,
THE SELWOOD PRINTING WORKS,
FROME, AND LONDON.

AUTHOR'S PREFACE.

My paper on "The Relation of Wages and Hours of Labour to Production" appeared in 1875, originally in the first half of the fourth annual volume of Holzendorff's *Jahrbuch*, and afterwards as a separate pamphlet. It was a tract for the times, inspired by a speech of Minister of Finance Camphausen, in the Reichstag, and the corresponding rescripts of the then Prussian Ministry of Commerce. The contradiction with which I was met led me to a further inquiry, entitled "The miners' out-put, particularly in Prussia, and the rise of wages dating from 1872," which appeared in the second half of the fourth annual volume of Holzendorff's *Jahrbuch* in 1876. This second article only supplied additional confirmation of the results of the first one.

Since then I have kept the question constantly before me and have accumulated a large quantity of material from the past as well as from the present. All this could only lead to the deepening and widening of the theoretical treatment of the subject. In proportion as my views developed, I regularly embodied them in my lectures (*cf.* Richard Faber, "The Rise of Agrarian Protectionism in England," Strasburg, 1888, p. 114); and I have had the great pleasure of being the means of stimulating two of my hearers, Dr. Gerhart von Schulze-Gävernitz and Dr. Ludwig Sinzheimer, to the further prosecution (in inquiries into the cotton and iron industries respectively) of my lines of thought. After the thorough-going confirmation which my views have received, not only from those inquiries, but also from the quite recent book of the American Schoenhof, and from the masses of material brought to light in all countries by the Eight Hours Movement, I may perhaps be permitted to regard them as permanently acquired to science.

In my lectures, the examination of the influence of wages and hours of labour on production forms the conclusion of a comprehensive inquiry into the effect on production of labour systems in general and of technical improvement. I do not overlook the fact that it is only in this connection that the examination in question becomes complete. If, nevertheless, I herewith publish it by itself, the reason is twofold. In the first place, years must necessarily go by before the publication of my Political Economy, while this particular question claims at present so large a portion of the public interest that an attempt from a scientific quarter to supply a clue to its difficulties may perhaps not appear unwelcome. In the second place, it would be impossible for a manual to adduce all the evidence, and to treat the question with the fulness which its great practical importance warrants.

In allowing the following inquiry to appear by itself, I cannot refrain from dedicating it to the memory of the man from whose lectures a quarter of a century ago I received the first inspiration of its fundamental idea.

L. BRENTANO.

Munich.

TABLE OF CONTENTS.

	PAGE
The Transformation in the Theory of the Relations between Wages and Production	2
The Change in the Economic View of Factory Legislation.	22
The Cause of this Transformation a Change in the Conditions of Labour	38
The Change on the Part of the Workman	89
Influence of Migration	41
Influence of the Increasing Competition in the World Market	46
The Increase of Production by Higher Pay and Shorter Hours, and its Limits	47
The Change on the Part of the Employer	49
Effect of the Diminution of the Hours of Labour on the Number of the Unemployed	69
Effect of the Rate of Wages and of the Duration of Labour on the Power to meet Competition	72
The Interest of the Nation and the Policy by which it can be Protected	75

APPENDICES.

A. Messance on the Effect of Cheap Years	79
B. Arthur Young on the Effect of Higher Wages on Production	87
C. The Effect of the Fall in Wages of 1874 on the Production of the Prussian Miners	88
D. Sir Joseph Crowe's Views on the Relation between English and German Production	89
E. Sir Lowthian Bell on Wages and Production	92
F. The German Iron Inquiry Commission of 1878-79 on the rise in Wages of 1872	99

PAGE

G. Senior on the Method of Economic Investigation . . . 101

H. Orthodox English Political Economy on Factory Legislation
in the Forties 102

I. Elijah Helm on the Present Position of the English Cotton
Industry 103

J. The Ship-builder, John Scott, on Hours of Labour and Production 104

K. English Firms which have Introduced the Eight Hours Day 105

L. Joseph Chamberlain on the Results of Shortening the
Working Day in his Works 106

M. The Agreement of 1892 about the Eight Hours Day in the
London Building Trade 107

N. Werner von Siemens on the Increase of the Labourer's
Requirements as the Condition of Larger Production . 107

O. On the Causes of the Transference of Cotton Spinning from
the North to the South of Lancashire 108

P. Number of Spindles and Consumption of Cotton per Spindle
in Great Britain and Ireland 109

Q. Table showing the Displacement of Child by Adult Labour
in the English Cotton Mills 110

R. Sir William Petty on the Results of an Increase in the
Income of the Poorer Classes 110

S. The Position of the Handloom Weavers working at Home in
the District of Zittau, according to Official Data . . . 111

T. Macaulay's Speech on the Ten Hours Bill (with special
reference to pp. 21 foll.) 115

THE HOURS AND WAGES OF LABOUR

IN REFERENCE TO PRODUCTION.

SOCIAL reform is the order of our day. The most important questions at issue at present are those of the organization of working men for the protection of their special economic interests, and of workmen's protective legislation—objects ardently longed for, clamorously demanded, keenly championed on the one hand, and on the other vehemently opposed.

What are the causes of this conflict? I will not go into all of them at present, but will confine myself in this place to one, the most important of all, insomuch as it exercises the strongest influence on the judgment, not only of the employer, but also of the good citizen—the menace, namely, supposed to be involved in such organization and such legislation, to the power of the country to hold its own in the market of the world. For, although undoubtedly the traditional views, feelings, and opinions of the propertied classes place many awkward obstacles in the way of economic and social progress, nevertheless they are comparatively easy to overcome, and would vanish of their own accord so soon as the one dread has been set at rest, that the rises of wages and the curtailments of work-time to which such workmen's organizations and workmen's protective legislation point, will so increase the cost of production that the home industry

B

will lose its power of competing with other countries in
the market of the world. To every one, therefore, who
has at heart the lasting prosperity and power of his
country, the relation of wages and work-time to production must be the Alpha and Omega of all questions of
social reform. I would invite the reader to enter upon
the consideration of these relations as impartially as
possible, in the objective spirit of the observer in a
physical science.

In the first place let us ask what science has to teach
us about this relation. And here we are met by a surprising transformation in theory when we compare the
writers of the seventeenth and eighteenth centuries with
those of the nineteenth. Houghton,[1] Petty, Temple,
Child,[2] and, in their earlier writings, Josiah Tucker[3]

---

[1] For a full exposition of the doctrines of Houghton, Petty, and
Temple, the earlier ones of Arthur Young, and the later ones
of Tucker, cf. Gerhart v. Schulze-Gävernitz, "Industry on a
Large Scale (*Grossbetrieb*)—An Economic and Social Advance :
a Study in the Field of the Cotton Industry."   Leipzig, 1892.
(Introduction.)

[2] Schulze-Gävernitz (*loc. cit.* p. 5) has erroneously reckoned
Child among Adam Smith's forerunners. Sir Josiah Child writes
in "A New Discourse of Trade" (Ed. 5, Glasgow, 1751, p. 12) :
" And for our own poor in England, it is observed, that they live
better in the dearest countries for provision, than in the cheapest, and better in a dear year than in a cheap, especially in relation to the public good, for in a cheap year they will not work
above two days in a week ; their humour being such, that they
will not provide for a hard time, but just work so much and no
more as may maintain them in that mean condition to which
they have been accustomed."

[3] Tucker had written in his " Essay on Trade," the first edition
of which was published in 1750 : "The men are as bad as can
be described ; who become more vicious, more indigent and

and Arthur Young, emphatically uphold the view that high wages are equivalent to low production. In order to increase exertion, either actual diminution of wages is advocated, or, what comes to the same thing, a raising of the taxes and of the cost of living. It is accepted as an axiom that the better off people are the less they work.[1]

About the middle of the eighteenth century a reaction begins to set in. In the first place the opposite doctrine first shows itself in the polemics of Vanderlint, Postlethwait, Forster and Tucker, and then we find it fully developed and supported in the work of Adam Smith. He maintains just the contrary, that high wages are equivalent to great production, and he bases this view not only on psychological and physiological grounds, but also on experience.[2] After he has spoken of "The common complaint that luxury extends itself even to the lowest ranks of the people, and that the labouring poor

---

idle, in proportion to the advance of wages, and the cheapness of provisions: great numbers of both sexes never working at all, while they have anything to spend upon their vices." Cf. an essay on "The Advantages and Disadvantages which respectively attend France and Great Britain with regard to Trade," by Mr. Josiah Tucker, of Bristol. 4th edition, Glasgow, 1756, p. 46.

[1] The most drastic presentment of these views is supplied by the author of "Considerations on Taxes as they are supposed to affect the Price of Labour of our Manufactures ; also, some reflexions on the general behaviour and disposition of the manufacturing populace of this kingdom : showing by arguments drawn from experience that nothing but necessity will enforce labour, and that no state ever did or ever can make any considerable figure in trade, where the necessaries of life are at a low price." 8vo, London, 1765.

[2] The discussion comes at the end of the eighth chapter of the first book of Adam Smith's "Wealth of Nations."

will not now be contented with the same food, clothing,
and lodging which satisfied them in former times"—a
complaint which might console many of those who lament
over the corruption of our own time—he says : " The
liberal reward of labour . . . increases the industry of the
common people. The wages of labour are the encouragement of industry, which, like every other human quality,
improves in proportion to the encouragement it receives.
A plentiful subsistence increases the bodily strength of
the labourer, and the comfortable hope of bettering his
condition and of ending his days, perhaps, in ease and
plenty animates him to exert that strength to the utmost.
Where wages are high, accordingly, we shall always find
the workmen more active, diligent, and expeditious than
where they are low ; in England, for example, than in
Scotland ; in the neighbourhood of great towns, than in
remote country places.   Some workmen, indeed, when
they can earn in four days what will maintain them through
the week will be idle the other three.   This, however,
is by no means the case with the greater part.   Workmen, on the contrary, when they are liberally paid by the
piece are very apt to overwork themselves and to ruin
their health in a few years. Excessive application during
four days of the week is frequently the real cause of the
idleness of the other three, so much and so loudly com-
plained of."

And after Adam Smith has taken occasion to pen a
diatribe against the short-sighted employers who drive
their workmen too hard, he emphatically controverts the
creed that in cheap years workmen are generally idler
than in dear ones.   A plentiful subsistence, it has been
maintained, relaxes, and a scanty one quickens, industry.
But even if there may be no doubt that this is correct

in the case of individual workmen, with the great majority it is false. That men in general should work better when they are ill fed than when they are well fed, when they are disheartened than when they are in good spirits, when they are frequently sick than when they are in good health, seems not very probable. The fact is that in dear years the workmen are far more dependent, humble, and submissive than in cheap years, the employers therefore make better bargains and have an easier time of it in the former than in the latter ; and so arises that point of view to the refutation of which Adam Smith goes on to bring some additional exact observations relating to the influence of more or less abundant wages on production.

Among these observations are systematic data furnished by the French tax collector Messance,[1] of St. Etienne. This author of " great knowledge and ingenuity," writes Adam Smith, has shown " that the poor do more work in cheap than in dear years by comparing the quantity and value of the goods made upon those different occasions in three different manufactures ; one, of coarse woollens, carried on at Elbœuf, one of linen, and another of silk, both of which extend through the whole generality of Rouen. It appears from his account, which is copied from the registers of the public offices, that the quantity and value of the goods made in all those three manufactures has generally been greater in cheap than in dear years, and that it has always been greatest in the cheapest and least in the dearest years. All the three seem to be stationary manufactures ; that is to say that, though their produce may vary somewhat from year to year, they are upon the whole neither going backwards nor forwards."

---

[1] See Appendix A.

Thenceforward the old view completely disappears from economic theory. As early as 1777 the reaction is evident in Anderson,[1] and even Arthur Young[2] and Benjamin Franklin[3] in their later writings emphasize the fact that low pay is by no means equivalent to cheap work, but rather the contrary. But it remained for two English economists of the thirties and forties—McCulloch namely and Senior—who are commonly regarded as in a special sense the theoretical upholders of the interests of the employers, to be the most emphatic representatives of the view laid down by Adam Smith.

McCulloch[4] speaks of the view of "many very intelligent people, of whose benevolence no doubt can be entertained, and to whose opinions on most subjects great deference is due," that high wages, instead of encouraging industry, usually become a fruitful source of idleness and dissipation. This opinion applies only to individuals, never to the masses. "Have the *low* wages," continues McCulloch, "of the Irish, Poles, and Hindoos made them industrious? or the *high* wages of the English, Americans, and Hollanders made them lazy, riotous, and profligate? Just the contrary. The former are as proverbially indolent as the latter are laborious and enterprising. This is not a point about which there can be any doubt. The experience of all ages and nations proves that high wages are at once the most powerful stimulus to exertion, and the best means of attaching the people to the insti-

---

[1] Cf. James Anderson, "Observations on the means of exciting a spirit of National Industry." Edinburgh, 1777, p. 351.

[2] See Appendix B.

[3] Cf. Roscher, I. § 173, note 3.

[4] McCulloch, "Principles of Political Economy." 5th ed., London, 1863.

tutions under which they live. It was said of old,
'Nihil lætius est populo Romano saturo;' and the same
may be said of the English, the French, and indeed of
every people."

Senior[1]—to quote also the man who invented the
term "wages of abstinence" for interest on capital,
and who at first was the ardent opponent of factory legislation—calls attention to the fact that high wage is by
no means the same thing as high price of labour. Senior
cites the evidence of English manufacturers who had
conducted business undertakings in France, to the effect
that in spite of the lower wages in that country, the
price of labour is higher and production more costly
than in England. The English workman, they explain,
produces incomparably more. In consequence of the
smaller production of the French, a larger number of
workmen is necessary for the manufacture of a certain
quantity of articles, and consequently more buildings,
more supervision—in a word, a larger capital on which
interest has to be paid. An Englishman, they said,
produces as much as two Frenchmen. Wages, continues Senior, are three times as high in England as
in Ireland, but the Irishman produces but a third of
what the Englishman does. "It may be supposed, indeed," he concludes, "that the price of labour is everywhere and at all times the same."

The conclusions of these English economists of the
first half of the present century are confirmed by the
following table,[2] which Houldsworth, one of the largest

---

[1] "Political Economy," 5th ed., p. 149 foll. London, 1863.

[2] From Schulze-Gävernitz, "Industry on a Great Scale"
(*Grossbetrieb*), p. 58.

living cotton-spinners, laid before a Parliamentary Committee:—

Year	A Spinner's Weekly Output.		Hours of Work per Week.	Total Wages.			Deduction for Assistants.			Net Earnings of the Spinner.			Purchasing Power of these Earnings in lbs. of Flour.
	Yarn Number.	Pounds of Yarn.		£	s.	d.	£	s.	d.	£	s.	d.	
1804	180	12	74·8	3	0	0	1	7	6	1	12	6	117
	200	9	do.	3	7	6	1	11	0	1	16	6	124
1811	180	18	74	3	12	0	1	7	6	2	4	6	175
	200	13½	do.	4	10	0	1	11	0	3	0	0	230
1833	180	22½	69	2	14	8	1	1	0	1	13	8	210
	200	19	do.	3	5	3	1	2	6	2	2	9	267

The English economists, however, of that period are not alone. Their German *confrères* also corroborate Adam Smith's doctrine by new observations. So we find J. G. Hofmann,[1] the father of Prussian statistics, showing that a Berlin wood-chopper does as much work in ten days as an East Prussian in Labiau in twenty-seven. William Roscher further says that a Mecklenburg day-labourer eats nearly twice as much as a Thuringian, but he also turns out nearly double the quantity of work, and in paragraphs 40 and 173 of the first volume of his "System," Roscher emphatically confirms and gives reasons for Smith's view. The Frenchman Michel Chevalier[2] holds the same relation to the latter as does Roscher.

Far more important, however, than all these detached

---

[1] Quoted from Roscher, I. § 40, note 1.
[2] Michel Chevalier, "Cours d'économie politique," I. p. 115.

observations is Brassey's[1] modern testimony, for Brassey was one of the largest contractors and employers of labour in the world. He built railways in every quarter—one might almost say, in every country in the world. He thus had ample opportunity of comparing the working-men of all nations, and must necessarily have acquired a wide knowledge of the price of labour in all countries. His son, Lord Brassey, who carries on his father's business, has published these experiences of his deceased parent in several works which have gone through a large number of editions. In one of these Lord Brassey says openly that he "feels himself impelled by many and potent influences to take the employer's view of the labour-question." This makes the testimony of this world-experienced man of business all the more important.

What, then, is this testimony ?

In his father's enterprises, in almost every country of the civilized world and in every corner of the globe, the price of labour was everywhere the same, whether wages were high or low; for when wages were low, the work done was correspondingly small. On the other hand, in those places where wages and work done were both small, the latter increased with the rise of wages, so that sometimes the price of work was cheaper after a rise in wages than it had been before. He animatedly repudiates the "allegations which, in times of commercial depression,

---

[1] Thomas Brassey, "Work and Wages," 2nd ed., London, 1872. "Lectures on the Labour Question," London, 1878. "Foreign Work and English Wages considered with reference to the Depression of Trade," London, 1879. Arthur Helps, "Life and Labours of Mr. Brassey, 1805–1870," London, 1872.

are invariably made, that our trade has gone to other
countries, because the wages of the British workmen are
excessive." The British export trade is, he says, continually on the increase, and the fact is that the greatest
increase has taken place in those trades in which the
wages are highest. It is not true that the price of labour
is higher in England than on the Continent. Thus the
Mülhausen printing-works import their cotton-goods for
printing mainly from England—a proof that such goods
are produced more cheaply in England, although higher
wages are paid in Manchester than in Alsace. He held
that the Hindoos constituted the sole exception; in their
case a rise in wages did diminish the work done.

Brassey's first work appeared in 1872—at a moment,
therefore, of the greatest economic change and of the
most considerable increase of wages in all branches of
industry and in all civilized countries. In 1873 came
the reaction. And then the accuracy of the judgment
we have quoted from Brassey was once more confirmed:
once more the workmen were made responsible for the
depression, and reductions of wages were recommended
as the best means of restoring economic health. This
opinion and this advice were even supported with all
the authority of his office by the then Prussian Finance
Minister, Camphausen, in the Bank Debate in the Reichstag, on January 26th, 1875; and the then Prussian
Minister of Trade, Achenbach, wrote as follows in a rescript of March 28th, 1876, to the Department of Public
Works, especially to the Administration of the Mines:
"At present the work done has remained not inconsider-
ably below that of former years, and it is just in the last
few years, in which the wages of the workmen have been
raised to a disproportionate extent, that the production

of the workman has almost without exception still further fallen off." If, therefore, under the present less favourable circumstances adequate profits were to be attained, it was necessary that the "production of labour should be increased, for the securing of which end an adequate lever is to be found in the lowering of the reward of labour."

Never, we may suppose, has an administration drawn from some few figures more untenable conclusions. At once the late Professor Erwin Nasse[1] made it clear that the protest instantly made by the miners against the assertion of the Minister of Trade was entirely justified. According to the official records, the year of the great rise in wages in the largest State mines, 1872, was followed by a considerable increase in the average output of the workman. These records showed the following figures (cwt.) in the case of the largest mines :—

	1871.	1872.
Saarbruck Mines	3,894	4,236
The King's Mine (Upper Silesia)	5,583	6,427
Queen Louisa's Mine (Upper Silesia)	5,111	5,290
Ibbenbüren	3,300	3,750
Osterwald	2,481	2,826

In the case of the far less important mines of Wettin, Löbejün, Borgloh-Œsede, and Deister, a slight diminution had, it is true, taken place; but this diminution, as I myself then exhaustively proved[2] from the official publi-

---

[1] *Concordia*, a weekly periodical on the labour question. No. 24, June 12th, 1875.

[2] Brentano, "The Output of Miners, especially in Prussia, and the Rise of Wages in 1872"; in Von Holtzendorff's "Jahrbuch für Gesetzgebung, Verwaltung und Rechtspflege," iv., Leipzig, 1876, pp. 402–409.

cations, had in the case of each of these mines its cause
either in the extension of constructional and mechanical
operations, in the working of less productive seams, or
in the employment of new and inexperienced workmen.
When, in the years 1873 and 1874, other mines also
showed a diminution of the average output, the same
causes were shown to be at work. In the annual reports
on the production of the individual mines published by
the ministry itself every year in its " Journal of Mining,
Smelting, and Salt Works in Prussia," this was in every
case adduced as the explanation of the falling off. Accordingly, the facts to which the rescript of the Prussian
Minister of Commerce appealed proved once more the
soundness of Adam Smith's doctrine, nor was the public
destined to wait long for an inverse corroboration of it.
Another official investigation, entitled " Contributions to
the Statistics of the Dortmund Mining District," by a
mining official named Hiltrop,[1] showed, in fact, that
in the above-named mining district the general fall of
wages in 1874 was accompanied by a diminution of production.

The facts in other countries provided Adam Smith
with a similar corroboration. In the report of the Liège
Mining Administration of May 19th, 1875, Chief Engineer
and Mining Director J. van Scherpenzeel-Thim drew up
a table giving the average yearly output and average
wages of the coal-miners in the province of Liège from
1830 to 1874.[2] Far from confirming his preconceived
opinion that a decrease of production accompanies an in-

---

[1] See Appendix C.

[2] " Rapport de l'administration des mines sur la situation de
l'industrie minière et metallurgique," 1874, p. 29. Cf. Brentano,
in Holtzendorff's *Jahrbuch*, iv. pp. 410, 411.

crease of pay, the table showed, to his undisguised surprise, that "the workman turned out most work when his pay was exceptionally high." In this case also deviations from this rule in certain years were explained either by a considerable increase of such preliminary operations as we have already referred to, or by the inferior productivity of the seams worked, or by an increase in the number of workmen. "It was necessary," he writes, with reference to the influence of the last-named factor, "to engage new recruits who had neither the experience nor the skill of finished miners, and this had naturally a depressing effect on the figures of the output averaged by each workman."

In the same way Theodor Hertzka's [1] estimate (based on official data) of the average output of the Austrian miner, showed that the rise of wages from 1872 in the Austrian mining industry, far from diminishing the average output of the individual miner, produced a very considerable increase therein. The figures were :—

Year.	Average rate of Exchange.	Average day's wage in silver reduced to Kreutzers.	Average yearly output of the individual workman in cwt.
1870	121·89	62·3	1,952
1871	120·27	70·7	2,079
1872	109·27	87·8	2,323

And in fact, proceeds Hertzka, how could the colossal increase of production which took place in 1872 in every department of industry in every civilized country in Europe have been possible but for an increase in the

---

[1] Published by Brentano in Holtzendorff's *Jahrbuch* iv. pp. 412–418.

average output of the workman which was itself due to
the increase in his wages ?

As is well known, all the civilized countries in the
world have, ever since May, 1873, been affected by the
industrial depression, which lasted till 1889, with the
exception of a short flicker of enterprise at the end of
the seventies. The consequence was that a Commission
was appointed in England in 1885 to inquire into the
causes of the industrial depression.

Those countries whose wages were higher than the
English suffered under the depression as much as those
where they were lower, the United States of North
America and the English colonies no less than the countries of the European continent. Only one would completely misapprehend the weakness of mankind were one
to anticipate that among the English manufacturers who
were heavily weighted by the pressure of the situation,
no single individual would be found to copy the example
of the German manufacturers and the Prussian Ministers
of Finance and Trade, and to characterize the high wages
of the English workman as the cause of the depression.
There is nothing to wonder at in that; what is remarkable, in comparison with the German proceedings we have
sketched, is that so many employers of labour should
have recognised at so desperate a moment that the
English workman's intensity of labour excelled that of
his less well-paid brother on the Continent to such an
extent that the Commission could say, in their concluding
report : " In our opinion the present state of trade and
industry cannot with a shadow of justice be attributed
to the action of trade-unions and similar combinations." [1]

---

[1] Final Report of the Royal Commission appointed to inquire

At the same time, however, certain points came up in
the evidence given by some of the most distinguished and
impartial witnesses before the Committee, which pointed
to an omission in the previous discussion of the relations
between wages and production. It is true that this
evidence too calls for a critical discussion.

This holds in particular of the evidence of Sir Joseph
Crowe, the commercial attaché to the English embassies
in Europe. His evidence rests evidently on the somewhat
doubtful information of others, and is uncertain and
evasive.[1] Even the evidence and the memorandum of Sir
Lowthian Bell,[2] the distinguished President of the Union
of British Iron-Masters, cannot be accepted without some
critical comments. Here also we find the repetition of
hearsay statements adopted without criticism, along with
comparisons between wages and production, which leave
out of account the differences in certain natural conditions of production, as, for instance, the varying richness
of the seams in coal-mines. Notwithstanding, Sir Lowthian Bell's evidence contains valuable personal observations of his own. He adheres strongly to Adam Smith's
doctrine and that of his followers, that higher pay entails
higher production; but you receive the impression that
in all trades in which manual labour is not, as it is in
mining, the exclusive agent of production, there is something besides the greater intensity of labour of the
English workman which counterbalances the lower wages
of the Continental and in particular of the German

---

into the Depression of Trade and Industry. London, 1886; xxi.
p. 84.

[1] See Appendix D.

[2] See Appendix E.

workman. We infer that there is yet another condition of production which, it is true, is connected with the greater productive capacity of the English workman and presupposes it.

In agreement with this evidence is the Report [1] which was issued a few years earlier, in January, 1879, by the German Iron-Inquiry Commission, composed of Chief Mining Director Serlo, Councillor Huber, Privy Councillor von Schlör, Baron von Stumm, and Consul H. H. Meier—men certainly free from any socialist tendencies. Here again also we find it emphasized as the unanimous opinion of experts, that the production of the more highly paid English workman must be counted higher than that of the German; here also a diminution of the workmen engaged in the iron industry without any corresponding diminution of production, and consequently with an increase of the product of the individual workman, is cited as a result of the rises in wages since 1871 ; here also it is proved that " Every rise in wages that is justified by the circumstances elevates both the power of production and morality," and a protest is raised against a reduction of wages as against a diminution of the productive power of labour ; but at the same time here also the increased capacity of production is not stated to be the exclusive cause of the increase in the average output of the individual workman.

Before, however, proceeding to state this cause, we must first of all mention here the most recent and comprehensive works which appeared in the course of 1892, and which confirm and complete each other in the most wonderful way. First came Gerhart von

---

[1] Appendix F.

Schulze-Gävernitz's book on Manufacturing Industry (*Grossbetrieb*), which showed admirably how, under the stimulus of increasing wages and falling work-hours, the English cotton industry has reached a degree of productivity which far surpasses that of all Continental peoples. A few months later appeared the book of the American Jacob Schoenhof, a manufacturer. In an inquiry into the cost of production of the foremost industries competing in the market of the world— an inquiry resting upon an astounding special knowledge—Schoenhof has exhaustively shown that the countries where lowest wages and longest hours prevail produce at the dearest rate, that the higher the wages and the shorter the hours the lower is the cost of labour in the individual countries; and that America, with its high wages, its worsted-yarn manufacture alone excepted, pays a much lower price for labour than England, let alone the continental countries of Europe. The following table gives a general view of the cost of labour in a series of the most important industrial products of America and England :—

COST OF LABOUR IN THE FOLLOWING LEADING ARTICLES.

	AMERICA.	ENGLAND.	OTHER COUNTRIES.
	Cents.	Cents.	Cents.
BROWN STONEWARE:			
Butter Pots—½-gallon, per 100.........	71.3	109	
„ 1 „ „	100	158	
„ 2 „ „	162	293	
„ 3 „ „	245	450	
„ 5 „ „	553	730	
„ 6 „ „	666	1,200	
FLINT GLASS:			
Bottles—16-ounce, per 100	88	91	
„ 2 „ „	42	58	
Decanters, 1 quart „	375	450	
Pitchers, 1 quart „	400	475	
Goblets „	130	127	
Tumblers „	95	80	
Finger bowls „	125	146	

C

			AMERICA.	ENGLAND.	OTHER COUNTRIES
			Cents.	Cents.	Cents.
Bituminous coal, gross ton			86	79	79 to 89 (Ger.)
,,	,,	(Penn., 1890)	64	..	
,,	,,	(Connellsv.)	33	(Durham) 51	
Coke-making	,,	,,	32	,, 24	
Iron ore	,,	(Lake Sup.)	119	(Staffordshire) 146	
Cheaper ores	,,	(Cumberl'd)	19	(Cleveland) 30	
Pig iron	,,	(East'n Pa.)	125	(Middlesboro') 73 to 96	
,,	,,	(Pittsburgh)	158	..	
Bessemer steel rails	,,	(East'n Pa.)	250 to 304	(Middlesboro') 307	
Cotton yarn, No. 20, per 100 pounds...			45	50	
,,	No. 40,	,, ,, ...	98	100	
Weaving print cloths	,,	yards ...	40	48 to 51	
4-4 Sheeting	,,	,, ...	45	50	
Worsted yarn, 2-40	,,	pounds ...	1,153	950	
6-4 WORSTED CLOTH :					
Weaving	per yard............		24.4	10.8	
Dyeing and finishing	,, ...		4.1	4.7	
6-4 WOOLLEN DRESS GOODS :					
Yarn	pound.................................		48	4	
Weaving	,, ...		9.8	7.4	
Finishing	,, ...		2.6	4	
6-4 Cheviot yarn, pound			3.9	4	
Weaving			7	4.4	
Carpets, yard.................................			4 to 5.25	4.5	
Silk throwing, pound........................			32 to 37½	40	
Weaving wages, yard........................			7	8.9	6 (Ger.)
Total, yard.....................................			18	13.9	15.25 (Lyons.)
Ladies' boots, pair			35	64	57 to 61 Ger.)
					71 (Austria).[1]

In direct opposition to these proofs and testimonies are the conclusions of the writers who preceded Vanderlint, Postlethwait, Forster, Tucker, Adam Smith, and the present-day complaints of the farmers, as well as the reports attainable on labour in India and generally throughout the East.

---

[1] This comprehensive table is to be found in Schoenhof's work, "The Economy of High Wages." New York and London, 1892, p. 347. In the comparison here given of the cost of labour in coal-mines, the varying richness of the seams is not taken into consideration any more than it was by Sir Lowthian Bell. Nevertheless, there is a difference between Schoenhof and Bell, inasmuch as the latter concentrates his mind exclusively upon the relation between the rate of wages and the rate of production, while Schoenhof on the other hand takes into account the other conditions which exercise an influence on the rate of production to this extent that he makes it depend on the rate of wages what seams are worked, and whether and to what extent human labour is supplemented by machinery.

How is such a conflict of opinion to be explained? I
will go into that question presently, but before doing so
will take a general view of the recent conclusions that
have been reached with respect to the relation, not now
of wages, but of hours to production. The circumstances
are quite analogous, and in both cases the explanation
is the same.

The workmen are at present clamorously demanding
that the working day be shortened; the employers offer
the strongest opposition from the fear that the change
may deprive them of their power to compete. There
is a last-century instance of the converse to this state
of things. At that time the working day in most industries was limited to twelve hours in summer and to
the hours between sunrise and darkness in winter. Such
were the conditions when, in 1777, Justus Möser,
in his "Patriotic Fantasies," wrote:[1] "Never have
I known a year in which every one was so hard working as last year. Circumstances compelled me to
build a new house, and although I was not in such a
great hurry myself, one and all hastened to place their
leisure hours at my disposal. Masons, carpenters,
joiners, even day-labourers gave me up the hours which
otherwise were devoted to their repose, and they expected, as was natural, that I should show my satisfaction
by a proportionate compensation. At first I thought
that I should be greatly the gainer; in the end, however,
I found it amounted to a swindle, and that every one who
was really working well, absolutely required his hours of
rest and recreation. Meanwhile, what was to be done?

[1] " Patriotische Phantasien," edited by his daughter, iii.
151. Berlin, 1858.

It was unadvisable to quarrel with the workpeople, and particularly with the artizans, who could injure me in other ways, and I let myself therefore be quietly cheated in order not to be cheated yet worse. As a matter of fact, however, the government ought to exercise a supervision in these matters, and altogether to forbid the labour of artizans in their leisure evenings, since it is merely a fraud both upon the regular master and upon the builder who gives their extra employment. This mode of cheating was unknown a few years ago, but it has daily grown more common ever since."

From this essay we can with certainty only infer the fact that towards the end of the eighteenth century efforts were made to lengthen the ordinary working day even in the building industry, and that so clever, keen, and far-sighted a man as Justus Möser recognised even at that day that this extension meant not an increase but a relative decrease of production.

Möser remained alone in this opinion. His contemporaries had another end in view.

Let the reader call to mind what was then in question, and what were the circumstances to be dealt with.

From the sixteenth century onwards a constantly increasing competition in the world market had grown up. The universal object was to beat competitors in the market of the world by the largest and cheapest production possible.

The working population was still entirely under the dominion of tradition. Not contract and the desire to secure by favourable stipulations the largest possible share in the national production, but status and the fact of belonging to this class or that, controlled the whole social and economic order. In many countries serfdom still existed, at least in the modified form of hereditary service and socage. In Catholic countries there was, moreover, the abundance of holy-days—an institution which before the days of freedom protected human dignity even in the serf. But wherever the remains of bondage existed there was also its corollary, *i.e.* the struggle of the workman to shirk his work and to idle as much as possible.

Then with the end of the eighteenth century came machine production. The amount of capital sunk in machinery was great, and the owner grudged every moment in which it was not used. The chief object was to redeem the invested capital as quickly as possible, and with this aim in view machines were worked as long as possible. This led to a prolongation of the working day to 19 and even to 20 hours. It was said by way of excuse that machinery had made labour easy which had been arduous; that it even rendered possible the employ- of little children where formerly grown-up people had been indispensable; and that as the work was no longer arduous, a prolongation of working days could do no harm. It was also maintained, on the ground that labour had been rendered a thing purely mechanical by machinery, that the last moment of the day's labour was just as valuable as any of the earlier ones.

The actual consequence of this easier but longer labour was a complete deterioration of the working classes, physically, mentally, and morally — especially of the women and children, whose labour replaced that of male adults. "And so it came to pass," to use the words of the first Sir Robert Peel,[1] "that that great achievement

---

[1] "Report of Evidence on the State of Children employed in

of British ingenuity, by means of which factory machinery attained to such perfection, became, instead of a blessing to the nation, its bitterest curse."

These evils led to the passing of labour legislation which lowered the working day in factories once more to 12, then to 11 and to 10 hours. Seventy-five years ago, operatives in the English textile industries were employed regularly from 90 to 100 hours in the week. The result of the different factory laws is that the working day now amounts to $56\frac{1}{2}$ hours per week only.[1] In most of the unprotected trades a like or even greater diminution has been brought about by the organization of the workers and the pressure of public opinion. In English mines in particular in 1842 the working day for all classes of labourers, women and children included, amounted to between 14 and 15 hours a day. At present women have completely vanished from the mines. In 1890 the miners' hours amounted to from 37 to 52 per week. Already most of the English mines have the 8 hours day, while in Durham the colliers work only $7\frac{1}{2}$ hours and in Northumberland only $6\frac{1}{2}$ hours from bank to bank.[2]

This movement enjoyed the sympathy of all men except the manufacturers and the political economists of the day.

Manufactures, 1816," p. 133. Cf. also John Fielden, M.P. for Oldham, and Manufacturer at Todmorden, in Lancashire, " The Curse of the Factory System." London, 1836.

[1] Cf. Sidney Webb and Harold Cox, "The Eight Hours' Day." London, 1891, p. 95.

[2] Cf. Return showing the average Number of Hours, etc., in and about Mines in the United Kingdom. Ordered by the House of Commons to be printed, July, 1890.

The English manufacturers of that time were short-sighted enough to oppose this movement, just as at an earlier period the German landlords opposed the abolition of villeinage, and as the German manufacturers of our own day oppose the factory legislation of 1891. If the relatively slight legislative protection which German labour has as yet obtained could provoke Baron von Stumm-Halberg in the German Reichstag to the winged word that we were nearing the point when we should, instead of a strike of employed, have a strike of employers, it is easy to imagine the indignation of the English manufacturers against the far more stringent English legislation. At each further curtailment of the working day, the latter demonstrated in the most positive manner that the proposed new limitation could not fail to rob them of all possible profit, to raise the price of goods, to lower wages, and to ruin the export trade. When the Ten Hours Bill was before the House of Commons, John Bright concluded his speech with the following passionate outburst: [1] "He would not detain the House farther; but believing, as he did in his heart, that the proposition was most injurious and destructive to the best interests of the country—believing that it was contrary to all principles of sound legislation—that it was a delusion practised upon the working classes—that it was advocated by those who had no knowledge of the economy of manufactures—believing that it was one of the worst measures ever passed in the shape of an Act of the Legislature, and that, if it were now made law, the necessities of trade, and the demands alike of

[1] Hansard, Parliamentary Debates. Third series, vol. 84, p. 1148.

the workmen and of the masters, would compel them
to retrace the steps they had taken ; believing this, he
felt compelled to give the motion for the second reading
of this Bill his most strenuous opposition."

Among the political economists this was a time of
unbounded faith in the all-saving power of *laissez-faire*.
Accordingly, their representatives in Parliament—
Joseph Hume, Dr. Bowring, Mark Phillips, Charles
Villiers, Labouchere, Roebuck, Baring, the younger
Ricardo, Lord Brougham, Lord Ashburton, and, after his
conversion to Free Trade, Sir Robert Peel—protested in
the strongest manner against this new encroachment of
the State upon the economic life of the country.[1] Outside
Parliament, Senior [2] at the same time pointed out that in
manufacture the profit was made exclusively in the
"last hour," and that to shorten the working day would
be tantamount to letting the machines stand idle.

In the meantime legislation for shortening the working day quietly went forward, and English industry, far
from being ruined, took a bound upwards at each fresh
law. Let us examine that classical subject of factory
legislation, the cotton industry. The figures are as
follows : [3]—

[1] Cf. "The Greville Memoirs," Second part, vol. ii., London,
1885, p. 236, where Lord Ashley and his Ten Hours Bill are in
question : "Melbourne is strongly against Ashley, and so of
course are all the political economists." Cf. also Macaulay's
Speech in the last Appendix to this volume.

[2] Cf. N. W. Senior, "Letters on the Factory Act as it affects
the Cotton Manufacture." London, 1837, 2nd ed., 1844.

[3] This table is taken from Porter's work "The Progress of
the Nation," London, 1851, and from the "Statistical Abstracts
for the United Kingdom."

Year.	No. of Spinning and Weaving Factories.	No. of Spindles for spinning.	No. of Spindles for doubling.	No. of Looms.	No. of Operatives.
1835	1,262	No infor-	No informa-	109,626	220,134
1839	1,819	mation.	tion.	No infor.	259,336
(In 1847 Ten Hours Act and prophecy of the downfall of the English cotton industry.)					
1850	1,932	20,977,017	No information.	248,627	330,924
1870	2,483	33,995,221	3,723,537	440,676	450,087
1874	2,655	37,515,772	4,366,017	463,118	479,515
1879	2,674	39,527,920	4,678,770	514,911	482,903
1885	2,635	40,120,451	4,228,470	560,955	504,069
1890	2,538	40,511,934	3,992,885	615,714	528,795

The number of spindles and that of operatives employed has thus almost doubled in the forty years since
the passing of the Ten Hours Act, while the number of
looms has more than doubled. The average size of
the factories has also almost doubled. In all these
directions the development has been continuous, and is
even now going on. In the light of such results we can
understand the scorn with which Dickens gave expression to the public opinion, which all the prophecies
of the manufacturers could not prevent from becoming
general :—

"Surely there never was such fragile china-ware as
that of which the millers of Coketown were made.
Handle them never so lightly, and they fell to pieces
with such ease that you might suspect them of having
been flawed before. They were ruined, when they were
required to send labouring children to school; they were
ruined, when inspectors were appointed to look into their
works; they were ruined, when such inspectors considered it doubtful whether they were quite justified in

chopping people up with their machinery; they were
utterly undone, when it was hinted that perhaps they
need not always make quite so much smoke. Whenever
a Coketowner felt he was ill-used—that is to say, whenever he was not left entirely alone, and it was proposed
to hold him accountable for the consequences of any of
his acts—he was sure to come out with the awful menace,
that he would 'sooner pitch his property into the
Atlantic.'   This had terrified the Home Secretary
within an inch of his life, on several occasions. However,
the Coketowners were so patriotic after all, that they
never had pitched their property into the Atlantic yet,
but, on the contrary, had been kind enough to take
mighty good care of it. So there it was in the haze
yonder; and it increased and multiplied."[1]

So far as the political economists are concerned, however, nothing can better show the transformation that
has since set in than the attitude of those modern representatives of economic theory, who make the defence of
the old orthodoxy their special business. They even try
to explain away John Bright's opposition to the Ten
Hours Bill, by saying that he was merely of opinion
that "so long as the price of bread was so dispropor-
tionately high as it then was, the first thing to do was to
get rid of the tax on wheat, before reducing the working
day,"[2]—the only misfortune being that John Bright's
above-quoted speech was not made till after the Corn
Laws had been repealed!

Unlucky Mr. Senior may be dismissed with the remark

---

[1] " Hard Times," chap. xvii.
[2] Minutes of evidence taken before the Royal Commission on
Labour (sitting as a whole); Professor Marshall's question to
Mr. Webb, queries 4217 and 4218.

that any one who could say as he did that, unlike the representatives of other sciences, the political economist has no need of tedious observations, but while mentally promenading at his ease, can from a few general premises deduce eternal laws, cannot pass for a representative of political economy;[1] and that favourite popular authoress, Miss Harriet Martineau, is simply to be set aside as a muddle-headed person.[2] It is certainly not my business to defend either Senior or Miss Martineau, but have the other English political economists of the thirties and forties followed a different method from that of Senior?[3] Did not Joseph Hume, the friend of Ricardo, then pass for a recognised exponent of political economy in the House of Commons? Has any one of the "recognised" English political economists of the thirties and forties spoken outside of Parliament against Senior and in favour of factory legislation? Do not the *Edinburgh* and the *Westminster Reviews* pass for the classical exponents of the economic orthodoxy of that day; and did not the former, so far back as 1846, designate the factory legislation we have described, as a "partial return to the system of slavery"?[4] Did not John Stuart Mill[5] wish to confine workmen's factory legislation entirely to children, and exclude women from it? And, so late as 1886, did not Professor Bonamy Price, as a member, though an isolated one, of the Royal Commission of Inquiry into the Decline of Trade and Commerce, use all the arguments of the orthodox political economy in

---

[1] *Ibid.*

[2] *Ibid.*

[3] Appendix G.

[4] Appendix H.

[5] Cf. John Stuart Mill, "Political Economy," Bk. V. ch. ii. § 9

his protest against shortening the working day by factory legislation? [1]

Professor Marshall goes even further in his apologetics. He declares [2] that Senior's opinions on factory legislation must not be ascribed to the classical political economy, any more than the barbarities perpetrated by the Spaniards in Mexico under the name of religion are to be ascribed to Christianity. At such a defence that classical political economy might well exclaim: "Heaven preserve me from my friends." For no criticism proceeding from their opponents could pass a more drastic judgment on the fanatical dogmatism of the classical political economists of the thirties and forties, than is passed by the employment of this familiar apologetic argument on behalf of economic orthodoxy. Meanwhile, though, in view of the evidence we have supplied as to the point of view then held by the rest of the English political economists, the fight which Marshall makes to cover its retreat cannot rescue the economic orthodoxy of the thirties and forties, nevertheless, it is a welcome sign of the extent to which political economy since Senior has learnt from experience, and of the nature of that experience. To be just, however, we should add that Senior himself, not less than John Stuart Mill, had a share in the transformation. When in the sixties the further extension of English factory legislation was in question, Senior declared [3] one of the most important tasks of social re-

---

[1] Cf. "Final Report of the Royal Commission on the Depression of Trade and Industry," 1886, p. 42.

[2] Minutes of evidence taken before the Royal Commission of Labour (sitting as a whole), queries 4091–4093.

[3] Cf. "Transactions of the National Association for the Promo-

form to be that of extending the protection given to
children by the factory laws to those branches of trade
which were as yet unprotected.

What, however, were the experiences which brought
about this transformation?

Before the passing of the Ten Hours Act, individual
manufacturers who were agitating for that law had set on
foot experiments in their factories,[1] with the view of testing
the assertion that the lowering of the working day from 12
10 hours would ruin the cotton industry. These cases
made it quite clear that the question was not merely the
arithmetical one,—if 12 hours produce x, what will 10
produce? It was found that the work done in the last
two hours was so small that in the experimental shortening of the working day from 12 to 10 hours the output
was not one-sixth but only one-twelfth less than formerly.
In addition to this, it was found that just in those last
two hours a good deal of material was spoiled by the
wearied and therefore careless operatives. When, therefore, the Ten Hours Act was actually passed, in spite of
all the opposition of the manufacturers and the orthodox
political economists, it became generally apparent that, as
Ernest von Plener said in his work on factory legislation,[2]
" The mere lengthening of the working day of a workman
was not equivalent to the increase of his productive
capacity ; the operatives, especially the younger ones, no

tion of Social Science, Edinburgh meeting, 1863." London, 1864,
pp. 67, 68. Cf. also Appendix 7.

[1] Thus, for instance, Gardiner in Preston, Fielden, but others
as well. Cf., for instance, Alfred, "History of the Factory Movement." London, 1857, II. pp. 247, 276, fol. and *passim.*

[2] Plener, "Die Englische Fabrikgesetzgebung," Vienna, 1871,
p. 93.

longer exhausted by excessive bodily effort, produced the
same amount, and frequently even turned out more in
the shorter time, having, owing to the almost universal
system of payment by the piece, a special interest in
doing so; and by degrees the employers themselves
admitted that the last two hours, formerly considered indispensable, used generally to produce work far inferior
to that of the preceding hours, and that owing to the
greater industry of the workmen, who no longer idled
through the first hours of the day, the regular, unbroken
labour of the new working day was much more advantageous to the employer than the longer working day
with its alternations of overwork and indolence." So it
came about that, as a result of the curtailment of the
working day, production not only did not diminish but
actually increased.[1]

The consumption of raw cotton in England amounted
to—

1846-50 ...	...	...	...	531,680,000 lbs.
1851-55 ...	...	...	...	748,250,000 „
1871-75 ...	...	...	...	1,279,380,000 „
1881-85 ...	...	...	...	1,138,910,000 „

The export of cotton fabrics from England amounted
to—

1846-50	...	25·33 millions of pounds sterling.		
1851-55	...	31·84	„	„	„
1888	...	70·54	„	„	„

The consequence of these brilliant results was the
cessation of all opposition on the part of the manufacturers, when in 1876 the English Factory Laws were

---

[1] " Report of the Commissioners appointed to inquire into the
Workings of the Factory and Workshop Acts." London, 1876,
vol. i. p. 11.

codified. "The progress of industry," as the Commission entrusted with this inquiry reported, "was evidently quite unhampered by the Factory Laws, and only a few employers now desire a repeal of the main clauses of those laws." If, however, the English cotton industry has recently been loudly complaining of the growing competition of India, the reason of this competition does not lie in the cheaper labour cost; on the contrary, the organ of those chiefly interested, the Manchester Chamber of Commerce,[1] reports that, in spite of the low wages in India, and of the fact that the working hours in Bombay are 80 per week, against 56½ in Lancashire, spinning in England is considerably cheaper than in India. India has, however, two extraordinarily important conditions on her side; she grows the raw material consumed by the textile industry, and she has the market for her production at her door. This means for the Indian spinner, in selling to the Indian market, an advantage of 1*s.* 3*d.* over England, and in selling to China an advantage of almost 7*d.* per lb.[2] In spite, however, of this Indian competition, the English cotton trade is ever advancing,[3] and the demand now put forward by short-sighted English manufacturers that their competitors should be subject to the same factory legislation as themselves would, if granted, only increase instead of weakening the Indian power of competition.

The experience of the English textile industry, that

<hr>

[1] Cf. the testimony of the Manchester Chamber of Commerce, given in Hallet; "Development of our Eastern Markets for British Cotton Manufactures," in the Annual of the Co-operative Wholesale Societies for 1890, p. 348.

[2] Cf. the same testimony in Hallet, *loc. cit.,* p. 349.

[3] Appendix I.

the curtailment of the working day leads to an increase in the national production, has been proved true
in other branches of industry and in all countries.
What other causes are at work besides the workman's
increased power of production, we have still to inquire.
But first we will endeavour to acquaint ourselves with a
few of these further experiences.

It has been everywhere observed that the workmen in
countries where work-time is short produce more than
in those where it is long. The relation of work-time to
production is exactly the same as that of wages to production. "In England," writes Schoenhof,[1] "I frequently heard it said, that labourers brought from Ireland
usually break down after the first week's trial; had then,
living with friends, to first get used to the English standard of life, and feed up in order to be able to do work
at the English rate." It is precisely the same with
work-time. An anarchist, who was taken into cus-
tody on his return from America, related, when ques-
tioned before the Leipzig Court in 1890, that it had
taken him more than a yéar, when he first went to
America, to hold his own in working with American
workmen. English workmen are wont to laugh at
French labour, calling it play;[2] and an English shipbuilder, who had pledged himself to build a portion of
the ships he had undertaken for that Government in
France in 1886, pointed to their longer working-hours
as the cause of the inferiority of the French workmen
compared with the English.[3] I myself was told in

---

[1] Cf. Schoenhof, "The Economy of High Wages," p. 30.

[2] Cf. the extremely characteristic evidence collected by Senior,
"Political Economy," 5th ed., London, 1863, pp. 150 foll.

[3] Appendix J.

March, 1890, by an overseer in Mr. Mather's machine works in Salford, and in the presence of a member of the firm, that he had worked in Dresden, England, and America; and he said that the greater efficiency of the American workman was a result of his shorter hours. In the same way he had observed an increase of production in Salford as often as the work-time was shortened; in Saxony, on the other hand, one of the chief reasons of the inferior efficiency of labour was the length of the working-day. From the lips of the deceased Emile de Laveleye I heard words of amazement at the slowness of the German workman as compared with the Belgian and the French; and with that opinion the reports issued by the German Iron Commission of 1878 agree.[1] The Indian cotton-spinners, likewise, have calculated [2] that the production of the English workman is to the production of the Indian as 56 to 23·2; and Brassey [3] says of the Russians, that one English workman produces as much in ten hours as two Russians in sixteen.

In complete harmony with the above, it has been further observed that in one and the same country, workers with regularly short hours outstrip those who regularly work longer; and a multitude of new observations has been made upon the increase of the efficiency of labour consequent upon further curtailments of the working-day. In each of these cases Brassey supplies numerous proofs; but it must not be supposed that similar observations have been wanting since the appearance of Brassey's work. After the passing of a Ten Hours Act in Massachusetts

---

[1] Appendix F.
[2] Cf. *The Economist* of January, 1889.
[3] Brassey, "Work and Wages," p. 144.

the well-known free-trader, Edward Atkinson, brother of the director of the largest cotton-spinning manufactory in Lowell, declared before a Parliamentary Committee that the Ten Hours Act of 1874 " was injurious to their working men, as they had to work for one-eleventh less than the similar workers in other States." Thereupon the Board of Labour Statistics was commissioned to make inquiry into the matter. In its Report [1] for 1881, the result of the inquiry is given in detail. Its conclusion was as follows : " It is clearly proved that Massachusetts with ten hours produces as much per man, or per loom, or per spindle, equal grades being considered, as other States with eleven hours or more ; and also that wages here rule as high, if not higher, than in the States where the mills run longer time." In the same way Donald reports an invariable increase of production by a tenth,[2] as the result of the introduction of the eight hours day in different industries in New York State. In Australia the eight hours movement, in 1858, began in the building industry in Melbourne. " It was powerfully promoted by Mr. James Stephens, a contractor, who showed, according to experiments made in his brick-works, that his people produced as much in eight hours as in ten." [3] From that time up to 1891,

---

[1] Printed in Sidney Webb and Harold Cox's " Eight Hours Day," p. 98.

[2] The inquiry was conducted by Charles F. Peck, Labour Commissioner for New York State. " To the question, ' Did the reduction in the number of hours result in the increase of the working force?' the invariable answer was that the increase was about one-tenth." *Economic Journal*, vol. ii., London, 1892, p. 552.

[3] Cf. Stephen Bauer in "Conrad's Jahrbücher für Nationalökonomie und Statistik," 3rd series, vol. ii. p. 648.

the eight hours day was extended to sixty industries, *i.e.*
to more than three-fourths of the working population,
without any injury to trade.[1] Nor is the general experience of Europe a different one. In reference to the
English coal-mines, Professor Munro[2] writes: "The
reduction in the hours of miners during the last fifty
years has been very great, and, though it has occurred
during a period in which many legislative restrictions
have been placed on mines, yet the production of coal
has steadily increased. In 1854, the output was sixty-
four million tons; in 1889, it was one hundred and
seventy-six million tons. It is quite evident from these
figures that any tendency towards a decrease of the output arising from the action of the legislature, or the
reduction of hours, has been altogether counterbalanced
by other forces tending to increase the output. There
is no reason to suppose that the operation of these forces
has come to an end." At the Congress of Hygiene at
Vienna, in 1887, the Swiss factory inspector, Schuler, reported that in Switzerland experience had shown that the
legal reduction of the working day from twelve to eleven
hours, *i.e.* by $8\frac{1}{2}$ per cent., had led, in short, to a falling
off in the less well-equipped cotton-spinning factories
of only 3 per cent. in production, while in the well-
equipped ones it was only 2 to $1\frac{1}{2}$ per cent. In
Mülhausen, Dollfus reduced his working-day from
twelve to eleven hours, and promised his operatives
that their wages should remain unaltered if they produced the same quantity of work as before. At the

---

[1] Cf. John Rae in *Economic Journal*, vol. i. p. 16 foll.

[2] Cf. Prof. J. E. C. Munro, "The Probable Effects of an Eight
Hours Day on the Production of Coal and the Wages of Miners."
Economic Journal, i. p. 248.

end of a month it was seen that not only as much work
was done in eleven hours, as formerly in twelve, but 5
per cent. more. But I will not repeat cases that have
been already discussed *ad nauseam.*[1] I will only add,
therefore, two quite recent instances. In the report of
the Stuttgart Chamber of Commerce of 1890, we find on
p. 47: " A corset-factory reports: ' Five years ago we
returned to a ten hours working-day (with a half-hour
pause in the morning, and another in the afternoon),
having previously worked our hands eleven hours and
more ; and we find that our work-women can get through
very much more with regular work for ten, or even nine,
hours than when the working-day is longer.' " Further,
early in September, 1892, a letter of Mr. Allan, proprietor of the machine works known as the Scotia Engine
Works in Sunderland, went the round of the English
papers, in which the writer stated[2] that the introduction
of the eight hours day into his business had resulted in
increased production by his workmen.

All this enables us to understand how it is that one
reads every day[3] of industrial establishments of every
kind—chemical works, machine works, printing works,
vinegar factories, shipyards, steel foundries—in England
and America which are introducing the eight hours day,
and, as a rule, double shifts as well ; nor is there anything

---

[1] A detailed conspectus is given in John Rae's Essay, entitled
" The Balance Sheet of Short Hours," in the *Contemporary
Review* for October, 1891, pp. 499 foll.

[2] The letter is printed in Hadfield and Gibbins's book. " A
Shorter Working-Day," London, 1892, pp. 170–180. Cf. also
William Allan's evidence before the Labour Commission.
Minutes of evidence (sitting as a whole), queries 6,857–72.

[3] See Appendix K.

strange in the fact, that at the end of October, 1892, one of the largest machine manufacturers in England, the above-named Mr. Mather, published [1] an essay to show how an eight hours day was to be brought about, and that his firm, Mather & Platt, in Salford, on the 20th February, 1893, introduced the eight hours day, as an experiment for one year, into their works ; or that Mr. Chamberlain, leader of the Unionist Party in England, and himself formerly a manufacturer, has made the legal eight hours day a part of his programme ; [2] or that the Munich *Allgemeine Zeitung* of November 7, 1892, published a London telegram to the following effect: "The men engaged in the building trade in this city, about 100,000 in number, are working eight hours for the first time," [3] or that at last even in Germany some firms are beginning to make experiments with an eight hours day. [4]

We thus see that the view which Möser expressed so far back as 1777, is borne out by experience. We see further that work-time and production bear the same relation to one another as wages and production. The facts we have cited have shown us that high wages and short work-time go hand in hand with far more intensive production.

Now how are we to explain the fact that the seven-

---

[1] Cf. William Mather, M.P., "Labour, and Hours of Labour," *Contemporary Review*, November, 1892. Cf. also the earlier paper of the same author, "Trade Unions and the Hours of Labour," Manchester, 1892.

[2] See Appendix L.

[3] See Appendix M.

[4] Cf. Dr. Otto Pringsheim in Braun's *Archiv für soziale Gesetzgebung und Statistik*, vol. vi. p. 14.

teenth and eighteenth centuries asserted the exact contrary ? How are we to explain the fact that even the
writers of to-day take the old view as regards Russia,
India, and the East generally ?   How is it that even
to-day we so often hear the exact contrary from practical farmers, especially in north-eastern and south-
eastern Germany ?

Ever since I first began to examine the relation of
wages and hours to production, eighteen years ago, I
have directed my attention to the answer to be given
to this question. My lectures have caused one of my
disciples, Herr von Schulze-Gävernitz, to undertake the
investigations published in his book on "Industry on a
Great Scale" (*Grossbetrieb*), which by the exact demonstration of the truth in question in relation to one particular branch of industry, has permanently won for science
the ideas I myself had been able only imperfectly to
substantiate, and in which the theory is worked out in
detail by a series of wholly independent arguments.
Schoenhof's work, which appeared soon after, and to
which allusion has already been made, then supplied a
comprehensive confirmation of the soundness of our view,
while a like service was rendered to it by observations
in Australia, and in a series of English and German
industries.

At the same time our solution of the contradiction
between the former and the present view will call attention to the limits within which the results of the experience we have cited can claim validity.   The fact is that
this contradiction finds its explanation in the transformation which has come about in the conditions of labour,
a transformation which has shown itself in the case of
both workmen and employers.

Let us first consider the transformation on the side of the workmen, and begin with a concrete case from real life.

At Meran and in the neighbouring country there are 130 holidays in the year, and the people have seven meals a day; yet it cannot be said that they make use of their favourable material condition and their large amount of leisure for an exceptional development of their personality. With them everything is traditional—the people's requirements and the work they do, their wages and their leisure. An increase of wages and of leisure would not in their case lead to an increase of production. Their requirements would remain unchanged, there would only be still more idleness, as it would take less trouble to satisfy the traditional standard of their needs.

It was just the same with the English workmen as described by Houghton, Petty, Child, and others, in the seventeenth and first half of the eighteenth centuries. They were still wholly under the dominion of custom. Again, it is just the same with the workers of the East, and of other climates, where custom and a low standard of requirements give the economic life of the lower classes its character. It is the same, again, with the labourers in our backward country districts; indeed in this case, owing to the fact that migration to the industrial centres leaves only the refuse of the labourers for agriculture, the state of things we have described is exceptionally prominent and serious.

As regards the English workmen of the seventeenth and beginning of the eighteenth centuries, the view of Petty and the rest was thus quite sound, just as a similar view still is for the workman of the East or of our own backward country districts. But, on the contrary, as we have seen, it is not sound for the modern workman, and the change which has come over him has been and is everywhere produced by the fact that the pressure which the progressive economic development has exercised upon his personal circumstances has pushed him out of the traditional rut as regards alike his requirements and his productiveness. But it is not without difficulty that this change is brought about. As Dr. Samuel Johnson (Works, viii. 218) has said: "Established custom is not easily broken, till some great event shakes the whole system of things, and life seems to recommence upon new principles." This great event comes about for the working man :—

Either (1) by his leaving home, and by the consequent necessity imposed upon him of gaining his living under entirely new conditions;

Or (2) by the pressure exercised on his energy, while he remains at home, by the growing competition and division of labour, in proportion as his own individual economic life becomes more and more involved with and absorbed into the economy of his nation and of the world.

The influence exerted by the renunciation of his home and of his accustomed surroundings in awakening the whole energy of a man may be gathered from the following facts.

Mackenzie Wallace [1] tells us that the Russians are extremely conservative, so long as they are left in their original moral condition. But even the Russian peasant, when transferred by circumstances into a new sphere of activity, makes no difficulty, he says, about accepting

---

[1] Cf. D. Mackenzie Wallace, "Russia," chap. xxxi.

whatever he sees to be to his advantage. In agriculture it is extremely difficult to bring about a change in his methods, even though it may promise him more. If, however, they gave up agriculture altogether, and went into the town to devote themselves to manual labour, as did many peasants under the Obrok system even in the days of serfdom, then they found themselves in a new world, in which none of their traditional ideas were applicable. Then there was no hesitation on their part to adopt new ideas and inventions; indeed, they soon surpassed the Germans in active energy. Here we have the explanation of the contradiction between the descriptions of Russian peasants in the novels of Slatovraczky and Ouspensky respectively, both of which are declared by competent Russians to give an exact picture of the facts.[1] The first describes a peasant who clings to the old order, the other a peasant who has broken loose from it.

We get just the same lesson, only still more impressively, from Kärger's book on migratory labour in Saxony.[2] Labourers from Prussian Saxony itself, and from the immediately neighbouring provinces, are no longer available for the beetroot-growers of that province. The natives stream off to the urban industries, in which they get better wages, and their place then is taken by imported labourers, chiefly from Upper Silesia. The latter have the worst possible character for idleness at home. Allured by the comparatively high wages offered them in Saxony, they migrate thither; and there, in a strange land they begin work early and leave it late, while

---

[1] Cf. Kovalevsky, "Modern Customs and Ancient Laws of Russia." London, 1891, p. 62.

[2] Cf. Karl Kärger, "Die Sachsengängerei." Berlin, 1890. Pp. 25 foll., 162 foll., 176 foll.

the savings they send home are extremely large. They amount to an average of £7 10s. in a beetroot season, and in exceptional cases rise to almost double that sum. It should be observed that these labourers rest as a rule during the winter, as they are then without work.

In this case the comparatively high pay, which for the Saxons themselves is an ordinary wage, and therefore no longer an adequate inducement to keep them in the country for the extremely fatiguing labour of beetroot cultivation, is the attraction that brings the Upper Silesians into the district and, after they have broken loose from their traditional circumstances, from idle these latter become industrious. We can observe the same thing also in the case of the Italians who year after year throng into all parts of Germany as navvies and stone-masons. That they are not always hard working in their own country is well known; and the fewer their requirements are when they are at home, the harder it is to move them to exceptional exertion. On the other hand, we are constantly amazed at the industry displayed, and the work accomplished, by the Italians who are employed every summer in Germany for a wage that we think a low one; and in their case also large savings are sent home. They stint themselves in every way they can. During the construction of the St. Gotthard railway there broke out among the Italian workmen an illness, the *pellagra*, of which the cause is insufficient food.

Observations of a similar nature from the colonies are recorded by Kärger in the passage we have already referred to.[1] No South Sea Islander, for instance, has hitherto ever been induced to enter foreign service in his

---

[1] "Sachsengängerei," p. 174.

own island. On the other hand, they let themselves be recruited in shoals to work in other islands in a thoroughly satisfactory manner.

Even with the highly developed labourers of our civilized countries we see the same thing. However much the production of the English workmen surpasses that of other Europeans, yet what they do at home is far behind what they do when they leave home and labour in the colonies; and thus the American labourer outdoes the English, and the Australian[1] the American.

As Kärger very justly says:[2] "To one who has torn himself away from the old life of the home, simply and solely with the object of earning money during a certain number of months by his labour, the mere fact of sojourn in a foreign country, among people who have all come there for a similar purpose, is alone enough to act upon him as an inner compulsion to more strenuous labour."

These facts suggest a view which might well be taken to heart in view of the agitation (extending even to a demand for the abolition of the freedom of movement altogether) for the limitation of the migration of labourers. For not only the consideration due to the workmen themselves, but also the permanent power of the nation to compete in the world's market, alike demand that the inclination for labour should become active among those masses of the population which have fallen behind in the race.

Yet the same change can also show itself among

---

[1] Cf. John Rae in the *Economic Journal*, i. 56, 41; and, further, the quotation in Hadfield and Gibbins' "Shorter Working Day," pp. 73, 74.

[2] Kärger, "Sachsengängerei," p. 175; cf. too the Duke of Argyll's "Unseen Foundations of Society," pp. 267-268.

the workmen who have stayed at home, the cause in their case being the pressure which the growing influence of international competition on their individual economic life exercises upon their energy, especially when they have the example of other immigrant labourers before their eyes.

Herr von Schulze-Gävernitz,[1] in his book on " Industry on a Great Scale" (*Grossbetrieb*), gives an excellent exposition of this development in the case of the English cotton operatives. When the first English factories were fitted with machinery, the natives of the present factory districts were still completely under the dominion of custom. They refused either to enter the factories themselves or to allow their children to do so. The necessary workmen had for the most part to be imported, and they consisted, moreover, of *déclassés* of all kinds; but when the competition of the new factories had more and more crippled the old domestic industries, the neighbouring population was content, not only to come itself, but also to send its children. Then began that terrible period during which the population of Lancashire was pressed deep below the standard of life to which it had been accustomed. When, however, the workman saw his old standard of life thus shaken and lowered, he set himself to work, not only to maintain, but even to improve it. And from that time onwards the supremacy of the English cotton trade in the world's market was assured. With a workman who was content with the old standard, such a supremacy was not to be attained, for there was no moving him to greater effort. Only with a workman who insisted

---

[1] Schulze-Gävernitz, "Grossbetrieb," pp. 61-65.

on the satisfaction of increasing requirements was it
possible to increase the speed of the spindles, to raise
the number of spindles he had to overlook, to diminish
the number of hands per spinning factory of a given size—
in a word, to bring about that enlargement of production
to which is due the fact that on the one hand, in spite of
short hours and lowered payment by the piece, the
weekly earnings of the English operative are the highest,
while on the other hand, in spite of those high earnings, the labour-cost of the English cotton industry is
the lowest in Europe. And now, on the contrary, let us
listen to a case in which it is found impossible to evoke
such an effort after a higher standard of living. That
excellent man, Commercial Councillor Frommel told
Herr von Schulze-Gävernitz [1] that he tried to persuade
the best weavers in his factory at Augsburg to work
three looms instead of two. The operatives objected.
When their attention had been called to the fact that
the new regulation meant higher weekly earnings, a
weaver replied that he and his wife earned £1 8s. the
week between them, and that he would not exert himself
to get more; more money a week only meant "more
booze."

The whole evolution is clear enough. In England the
change of the sum total of economic conditions in the
first place made the employers strive more than ever
for the greatest possible profit. The pressure thus
exercised caused a corresponding change among the
workmen. They had to adapt themselves to the new
conditions. Once sundered from old use and wont, they
too felt new needs; and now the workman, too, has set

---

[1] *Ibid.*, p. 66, note 1.

his face on the modern road, and the race begins between the growth in his requirements, which leads to
increased production, and an increase in production,
which in its turn leads to a growth in his requirements.
In cases, on the other hand, where the old order is
tenaciously adhered to, the technical progress which presupposes the increase of the efficiency of the labourer is
hindered by the most serious obstacles.[1]

The one explanation of the contradiction between the
doctrines of the economic writers of the seventeenth and
eighteenth centuries, the information available on
Eastern labour, and the statements of many of our
practical farmers on the one hand, and the recent experiences we have recounted in manufacturing industry
on the other, is to be found in the fact that the working class has changed. Man has always hated intensive
labour. Only necessity and the increase of his requirements,—the latter rising with the gradual rise of the
working classes,—have exercised a pressure adequate to
overcome this obstacle. On a lower stage of labour the
shortening of work-time lessens production in equal proportion, and the increase of wages diminishes the number of working days. But when, with the rise of the mer-
cantile system, the economic life of nations became in an
ever-increasing degree absorbed into one world-comprising
economic organization, competition necessitated the more
strenuous exertion of all faculties. This necessity has
reached at last the economic life of the working classes,
and in an increasing degree that life has become subject to
the desire for the greatest possible gain. The severance of
the workers from their accustomed circumstances has led

---

[1] Appendix X.

to an increase of their requirements, while the increase in their efficiency, due to higher wages and shorter hours has made it possible to satisfy them. So we get those increases in production to which we have referred. Where, on the other hand, agricultural workers still remain on a lower level than the rest of the population, and are still unaffected by the struggle we have described, in such cases the old view even now applies.

It is important, however, to guard against an error. Even in the case of the modern workman, every rise of wages and every shortening of work-time or improvement in the conditions of labour does not necessarily lead to an increase of production, but only those improvements which lead to an elevation of the standard of moralized life.

With this fact is connected the other one ; namely, that improvements in the conditions of labour that are of short duration have, as a rule, no effect, or no appreciable effect, upon the increase of the workman's production. For the first effect of a rise of wages is like the first effect of a material improvement in the condition of most men ; namely, prodigal waste by the workman of the larger income or the greater leisure he has obtained. If, however, the improvements last for some time, they will be employed on better food, greater care of health, more recreation, and of a more moralized kind, and higher education ; in other words, they lead to an increase of those physical and spiritual requirements of the workers which are in themselves desirable, that is, to the elevation of their whole standard of life.

It follows, further, that an increase in production cannot be brought about by a sudden upward leap in the conditions of labour. For the elevation of the standard of

moralized life in the case of workmen, as of all mankind,
cannot be brought about by leaps and bounds. The man
who seeks to attain a larger share of civilization must first
live into that larger share, and learn to enjoy it if he is
really to make it his own. Accordingly, in Germany, let
us begin, not with a general reduction to an eight hours
day, but with a ten or a nine hours day, according to the
individual trades.

Where, however, a rise in the standard of life has
come about as a consequence of increased wages and
shorter hours, experience shows that it induces greater
intensity of labour, since men whose requirements are
larger and their hours shorter are compelled to greater
industry, and that at the same time it makes that intensive labour possible, owing to the fact that favourable
bodily circumstances and greater pleasure in labour
make the greater industry easier to such workmen than
to those whose requirements are small, and who are
badly nourished, weary and depressed.[1]

That this development is to the interest of the
labourer needs no further demonstration. But no less
is it in the interest of the community, and not only in
its socio-political, but also in its economic interest, for
it is by this development that the preliminary conditions
are first created under which industrial progress becomes physically and economically possible.

This brings me to the second change in the conditions
of labour which explains the contradiction between the
present and the former view of the relation of wages
and hours to production,—to the change, namely, that
has come about on the side of the employer.

[1] Cf. Roscher, "System" I. § 173.

The above-stated effects of higher wages and shorter hours on the productive power of the workman are not enough by themselves to explain the increase of output which has coincided with the improvement of the conditions of labour. For there are employments in which the men work without machinery, like coal-hewers in mines, and in these cases it is by no means always possible to point to an increase in the total output exactly corresponding to the rise of wages or curtailment of working-hours. I have already mentioned that it is established by the testimony of Sir Lowthian Bell, and by that of the German Iron Commission of 1879, that higher wages do, it is true, increase the average output of the individual workman, but that at the same time the increase of production which is obtained is by no means always enough to outweigh the low wages which prevailed formerly, or which still prevail elsewhere. Exactly the same applies to the hours of labour. When, for instance, in 1871, in Northumberland,[1] the working hours of the coal-hewers were shortened 16·69 per cent., the output per hour certainly rose, but the rise was not sufficient to counterbalance the deficiency consequent upon the diminished number of working hours. The output per shift diminished to the extent of 6·78 per cent. In the same way, according to the German *Imperial Gazette* of February, 1891, the shortening of the hours of the coal-hewers in the State mines of Westphalia from ten and fourteen to eight, diminished the average output from 1,072 tons in 1888–89,—not, it is true, to 750 or 850 tons, which would have been the arithmetical equivalent of the shortening of the working

---

_[1] Cf. "Schriften des Vereins für Socialpolitik," vol. 45, p. 190.

E

day,—but still to 919 tons. Granted that in this case other causes co-operated (for without a further shortening of the working day the average output since then has fallen off another five per cent.), still these figures show that as in Northumberland, so also in Westphalia, the increased production per hour of the coal-hewer was not enough to make good the curtailment of the working day. Similar experiences have been recorded in all industries which have remained stationary as regards technique and economic organization,—for instance, the flax-spinning industry in Ireland,[1]—while the already mentioned utterances of Chamberlain [2] point to the same conclusion.

How is it then that, in other branches of industry, as the conditions of labour improved, there was an increase, not only in the production of labour per hour, but also in the total output?

Does the reason lie with the employers?

In so far as the greater production of the workman due to the increase of his wages does not counterbalance the former lowness of his wages, or in so far as the greater production due to the shortening of his work-time does not outweigh his former long hours, to that extent the improvement in the lot of the workman means in the first place a greater cost of production for the employer. This leads either to an advance in technique, either by being the direct occasion of invention, or by making the application of old inventions for the first time economically and physically possible, or again it leads to

---

[1] Cf. Second Report of the Royal Commission on the Depression of Trade and Industry. London, 1886 p. 261, qu. 7012, 7013.

[2] See Appendix X.

improvements in the economic organization which otherwise would not have been attempted.

I shall not linger over the commonplace, that necessity is the mother of invention. America alone, the land of the highest wages and the greatest progress in machinery, speaks volumes. We are inventors by necessity, cries Schoenhof,[1] in his exposition of the way in which high wages and short hours have helped to awaken the American spirit of invention.

But more important still is the influence of high wages and short hours on the practical application of inventions already known. It is an old-established economic maxim, to which the lectures of Hermann and Helferich in particular have given emphatic expression, that it is not the greater technical perfection of a process of production, but merely its greater cheapness, that settles its practical employment in industry. It is not enough to invent a labour-saving process of production to ensure its adoption; its application must cost less than the labour it replaces. So the first result of a rise of wages and shortening of hours is the practical application of better methods of production,[2] which from a purely technical point of view have long been possible. Conversely these perfected technical processes, in particular the faster, more delicate machines which with fewer workmen turn out a far greater production, are for the first time physically possible with superior workmen,

---

[1] Schoenhof, "The Economy of High Wages," p. 54.

[2] Cf. Dürre, "Katechismus der allgemeinen Hüttenkunde," pp. 69, 73 foll. "When wages are high," writes Dürre, "every effort is made to replace hand labour by machinery." Hand labour in industries of any size can only be retained where, in addition to low rents, "wages are not very high."

well paid, well fed, intelligent, strenuous, and eager.
Just as, in all countries, it was only after the emanci-
pation of the slaves and serfs that the use of better tools
and machines [1] became possible, so in the case of the
free workman the higher standard of life is necessary if
he is to handle and control those works of wonder which
now often complete in a minute the former work of
months and years. Thus high wages and short hours
are the occasion and condition of an increase in production by means of improved technique ; while, on the other
hand, where the technical development of nations is
inferior, we may look to low wages and long hours for
the cause.

Here, then, is the explanation of that wonderful cheapness of labour, combined with the highest wages and the
shortest hours, by which, as I have shown, America
excels even England, to say nothing of the rest of Europe.
"The law of gravitation," writes Schoenhof,[2] "is not
more absolute than this, that where, as in America, the
rate of wages of labour per diem is a high one, the first
object of the employer is to economize its employment.
The result is that in no country is the organization of
labour in mills and factories so complete as in the United
States. In no country is the application of machinery
carried to the extent to which it is carried in the United
States. Here invention and improvement are always
most readily welcome in the labour processes involved.
Manufacturers introducing a change in manufactures
have a machine built to accomplish what in other coun-

---

[1] Cf. Cairnes, " The Slave Power," Ed. 2, London and Cam-
bridge, 1863, pp. 53, 355 ; Roscher, " System," I. § 71.

[2] Schoenhof, pp. 33, 34.

tries would be left to hand labour to bring about.
Machinery, used to the limit of its life in Europe, is cast
aside in America if only partially worn, or while satisfactory in this respect, if an improvement has come out that
can do the work quicker, and consequently cheaper.
The improvement introduced by one manufacturer in
any line is quickly adopted by his competitors. Labour
saving is the result, and a cheapening of production en-
sues, which is the due outcome of the high cost of day
labour in the United States." But no less stress does
Schoenhof[1] lay upon the fact that these technical improvements can only be applied with the help of a workman whose capacity of production has been raised to
the American standard by high wages and short hours.
"The higher wage rate per diem," he writes, "ruling in
the United States enables the operatives to enjoy a better
mode of living, and better nutrition of body and mind.
They eat more and better food than any of the operatives
of Europe, and their general mode of living is upon a
higher standard.   They operate more spindles, more
looms in the textiles.   In steel-making, coal-mining,
coking, etc., an equal number of hands turn out more
tons in a given time than any of their competitors in
Europe, England not excluded.   They work more
steadily in every hour of their working day.   The steadi-
ness of the worker, the application of his whole time and
energy to his work, is most intense, and is only possible
where good nutrition prevails.   Every moment is made
use of to turn out the greatest number of pieces that can
be ground out of his machine, or run out of his hand
while at work. This alone explains the high rate of earn-

[1] *Ibid.,* pp. 84, 85.

ings in some occupations, coupled with the low piece-
price paid, which, when I stated it to manufacturers in
the same industries in European countries, caused aston-
ishment."

In the same way the influence thus exercised by high
wages and short hours upon processes explains the otherwise inconceivable productivity of Australian agriculture.
In his interesting work on the " Rural Economy of Australia," Robert Wallace [1] gives us a picture of the agricultural machines used in Australia.   For the most part,
the European continent has no notion of such machines :
ploughs which at one and the same time cut a seven-feet
furrow, pulverise the surface of the soil, and carry out
the process of seeding and rolling at a total cost of four
shillings per acre ; sheep-shearing machines, by means of
which the shearer's output is raised 20 per cent., and
which avoid at the same time the double cutting of the
wool.   As Wallace points out, high wages and nothing
else have led to the processes of production which have
thus increased the quantity of the work done and improved its quality.

Even in coal-mining we may, as Professor Munro [2]
shows, trace the effect of improved conditions of labour
on the advance in technical processes.   It is true that
coal-cutting machines are not used to any large extent ;
the moving of a machine from one seam to another, and
the supply of motive-power, cause too many difficulties.
A coal-cutting machine, therefore, is useful not so much

[1] Robert Wallace, " The Rural Economy and Agriculture of
Australia and New Zealand."   London, 1891, pp. 268-283,
377-380.

[2] *The Economic Journal*, i. 249, 250.

for increasing the quantity of coal produced as for turn
ing it out in a form which fetches a better price in
the market. It is in winding the coal to the surface,
rather than in coal-cutting, that the chief advances have
been made in the application of machinery to mines.
The extent to which these advances are possible is shown
by the fact that in one of the largest Lancashire collieries
in 1852 only 600 tons per day could be wound from
twelve pits, whereas now that quantity can be got in the
same time from a single pit.

"The average number of hours the hewers are at the
face, and the average number of hours the winding
machinery is in motion in the leading coal districts, are
as follows :—

	Average number of hours worked at face.	Average number of hours coal is drawn to surface.
Northumberland	6·07	4·50
Durham	5·87	5·30
Staffordshire, S.	7·32	7·6
Yorkshire.	7·5	3 to 5·25
Lancashire, W.	7·86	9·5
" N. and E. . . .	8·0	8·0
S. Wales	7·66	9·0

"It will be noticed from this table that in the three
first-mentioned districts, where the miners work the
shortest hours, and yet hew the largest amount per man,
the winding machinery and the methods of bringing coal
to the surface are superior to those found in other districts. In the northern counties and in Staffordshire the
coal can be brought to the surface in a shorter time than
it takes to hew it; in the other districts it requires a
longer time. The distance of the face from the surface

is not sufficient to explain these differences, as appears from an examination of the returns issued by the Miners' Federation. One is forced to conclude that the appliances and methods used for hauling coal in many coalfields are open to improvement."

This statement of Munro's about the English coalmines shows us the inferiority of collieries with worse conditions of labour compared to those with better ones; and the advance in the English iron works, as compared with the German, brings out the same result. According to Sir Lowthian Bell's calculations,[1] owing to the higher wages of the English puddlers, the cost of labour in the puddling process in 1879 was 145 in England as compared to 100 in Germany. The result has been extremely fortunate for English industry, as well as for the English working class. England has consequently set to work to oust the puddling process and replace it by the Siemens-Martin process far more energetically than has been the case in Germany. While in England the iron produced exclusively by puddling amounted to 32·3 per cent. only of the total malleable iron produced in 1890, in Germany it still amounted to 41·2 per cent.[2] The manual labour of the puddler in England has thus, to a far greater extent than with us, been replaced by mechanical processes which liberate the human being from one of the most exhausting of labours, and one, too, calculated to unfit him very soon for any other occupation, which put an observant and intelligent workman in the place of the man distinguished merely by physical strength,

---

[1] Appendix E.

[2] Cf. Wedding, "Statistik des Eisens" in *Stahl und Eisen,* 1892, p. 249.

and which increase production in a very marked degree. In Germany, however, this substitution was not equally possible, because the forging of the Martin material presupposes exceptionally skilled smiths, as unskilled smiths, in forging the Martin molten iron, often scorch the material, because they treat it as they would the ordinary malleable iron. Consequently, in Germany, we still retain the puddler, whose displacement, according to the iron-masters themselves, is strongly to be desired in the interests of humanity.[1] While the puddler is dying out in England,[2] we are contenting ourselves by replacing the simple old puddling oven by the oven with the double hearth, which, compared with the quondam puddling process, admits of a certain amount of saving in coal and labour. And so long as the wages of our puddlers are so much lower than those of the English, our puddling works will still survive. For, while that inferiority of wages lasts, the replacement of such works by something better is neither economically nor technically feasible.

It would, however, be an error to conclude from the foregoing that the only progress to which employers are induced by improvements in the conditions of labour is one in the technical processes of their industry. Not less effective are the improvements they are led to introduce into the general organization of their industry. Thus all employers who have already introduced the eight

---

[1] Cf. Ludwig Sinzheimer, " Der volkswirthschaftliche Character der technischen Entwicklung des deutschen Eisenhüttengewerbes, 1865–1879 "; Munich Inaugural Dissertation, 1891, pp. 43–71.

[2] Cf. Lotz in vol. 45 of " Schriften des Vereins für Socialpolitik," p. 272.

hours day dwell upon the great advantage that has accrued to them from it, from the fact that breaks for rest and meals can now be dispensed with. " Every break," writes one of them, Mr. Beaufoy, M.P., " causes loss of time in coming and going," and the rest say the same thing. In other cases the eight hours day led to the introduction of double, even of treble shifts. In some industries the profit was not only equivalent to the old one, but was increased, owing to the lesser cost of supervision, which in some cases was abolished altogether; while in others the same result was produced by greater concentration of the industry; and in others, again, by improvements in the means of transport of the material as well as of the manufactured goods, by the cheapening of the staple materials, as well as of the supplementary and auxiliary ones, and by improving the conditions of sale and market.

All these conditions co-operated with peculiar energy in the development of the English cotton industry. Schulze-Gävernitz has shown this thoroughly and clearly in the work we have referred to, and there is, in fact, hardly anything which throws more light on the effect of social advance on the prosperity of an industry than his comparison of the English with the German cotton industry.[1]

The thirties and forties of the present century were in England the days of the frightful conditions of factory labour which Engels' descriptions have made so widely known in Germany.[2] In 1847 the Ten Hours Act was

---

[1] Schulze-Gävernitz, " Der Grossbetrieb," pp. 46–212.
[2] Engels, " Die Lage der arbeitenden Klasse in England." 2nd ed., Stuttgart, 1892.

passed, and from 1850 onwards it was really carried out. In 1853 the great strike of cotton-spinners took place at Preston, which, though a failure, was important for the organization of the cotton-spinners. Originally the machines had been small, and had employed a large number of badly paid, badly fed, and yet, owing to their large number, expensive workmen. When the working day was shortened, it was not possible to face the growing competition of the world-market with such imperfect technique and wretched labour-power. What then has the development of the English cotton industry to show us?

Before all things it shows a concentration of factories on the places possessing the most favourable conditions for production. And what are these places? Those where wages are the cheapest? Among such was, for instance, Ireland, with a few spinning factories, employing about 3,000 hands at wages half as high as in England. But for that very reason, labour in that country was far too dear for English capital to seek investment there.[1] The place it chose was where the highest-paid labour gave assurance of the most energetic utilization of the other favourable conditions of production. Lancashire became the centre of the cotton industry, and even within Lancashire itself the industry tends more and more to leave the north, and concentrate itself upon the south.[2] The Irish cotton industry, with its cheap labour, came to an end altogether, and that of Scotland was limited to certain specialities.

So we get an increasing concentration of the industry into comparatively few works along with the elimination of all employers not well supplied with capital. The

---

[1] Cf. also Schoenhof, p. 41.   [2] Appendix O.

number of spindles and looms in England (cf. p. 25) doubled itself between 1850 and 1890, while that of factories only rose from 1,932 to 2,674 between 1850 and 1878, and then sank back again to 2,538 in 1890, though the number of spindles simultaneously increased.

Among themselves these factories show a tendency to increasing division of labour; each confines itself to a speciality in order to attain the greatest possible cheapness of production in it.

In the service of these factories an unceasing effort to improve the means of transport next confronts us, a development of commerce which aims at steadying, as far as possible, the fluctuations in the price of raw material, and at making money as cheap as possible, and a system of linking on to the great cotton centres those special supplementary industries which, like machine-making works, are merely intended to serve their needs; in a word, the utmost perfection in all arrangements conducive to the cheapening, not only of the raw material, but also of all auxiliary and supplementary materials.

But still more amazing and important is the technical progress in the inner working of the factory. In the spinning factories we find the number of spindles on a single frame trebled. Where formerly a machine could work 800 spindles at most, there are now self-actors of 1,200 spindles and more. The number of spindles in a couple of self-actors is 2,000 on an average. Add to this the much quicker pace at which the machines are driven; while the distance covered by the machine has risen from 58 to 65 inches, the time for an inward and outward run has gone down almost to half—in some counts nearly to a third. Whereas, in 1834, the spindles could only make 4,200 revolutions in a minute, their number has now risen to 9,000—in some cases as high as 11,000 ;[1] and whereas, formerly, the cotton had to be combed twice to clean it, a single combing now suffices.

In the weaving trade there were still 220,000 hand-looms in 1831; by 1856 they had gone down to a few thousand; to-day there are still a few hundreds of them left. On the other hand, the number of power or machine looms had not only risen to 615,714 in 1890, but each workman now manages 3·9 looms on an average; and the number of picks of the loom per minute, which in 1830 amounted to from 80 to 90, to-day amounts to 190, and has even reached 240.

To work of that kind, however, children were no longer equal. Whereas the total number of persons occupied in the cotton industry rose from 479,515 in 1874 to 528,795 in 1890, we find that the number of children went down from 66,900 to 48,133. The machine, while still imperfect, had substituted for the *paterfamilias* the labour of the child ; and every one has read descriptions of the father wandering about unemployed, or cooking the dinner and mending the stockings at home for wife and child, while they were at work in the mill. The perfected machine, on the other hand, makes the father once more the family bread-winner, and restores the child to the school to which he properly belongs.[2] Henceforward, grown men are wanted for the work, and, indeed, only such are of any use whom a higher standard of living has fitted to meet the higher demands made on them by the machinery. Thus has come into being the modern spinner, who, with his two helpers,

---

[1] Appendix P.　　[2] Appendix Q.

works 2,000 spindles at once; and the modern weaver, who keeps four looms going at once. The output per workman has risen from 2,754 to 5,520 pounds in the spinning, and from 1,658 to 4,039 in the weaving industry, in the years between 1844 and 1882, as the following tables will show :—

DEVELOPMENT OF ENGLISH COTTON SPINNING.[1]

	Yearly production of yarn lbs., 000 omitted.	Number of spinners.	Production of yarn per workman in lbs.	Cost of labour per lb. of yarn.	Average yearly earnings of the workmen.
				s. d.	£ s.
1844–46	523,300	190,000	2,754	2 3	28 12
1859–61	910,000	248,000	3,671	2 1	32 10
1880–82	1,324,900	240,000	5,520	1 9	44 4

DEVELOPMENT OF ENGLISH COTTON WEAVING.[2]

	Total production of cotton cloth in lbs., 000 omitted.	Number of weavers.	Production per workman in lbs.	Cost of labour per lb.	Yearly income per workman.
				s. d.	£ s.
1844–46	348,110	210,000	1,658	3 5	24 10
1859–61	650,870	208,000	3,206	2 9	30 15
1880–81	993,540	246,000	4,039	2 3	39 0

And not only has England gained a capable workman,

----

[1] In the table in the text, all yarn-counts without distinction are thrown together on the basis of the figures supplied by Ellison. Cf. Schulze-Gävernitz, "Grossbetrieb," p. 132.

[2] On the basis of Ellison's estimates in Schulze-Gävernitz. p. 149.

who, in spite of his high weekly earnings, is cheaper than any Continental workman, but she has also transformed a wretched helot, employed in the production of goods unattainable by himself, into a solvent customer for his own produce. This, however, is not the place to go further into the advantages bound up with the opening up of this new market; moreover, the point has already been strongly brought out by others.[1]

In contradistinction to England, Germany has, during scores of years, devoted herself to the protection of the economically unfit, instead of to the protection of the weak; and instead of seeking a basis for her competitive power in unwearying technical advance, has sought it in low wages and long hours. The consequence is that in Germany we find no concentration of works in a few spots; in the north and the south alike, manufacture is scattered over wide districts, and lacks commercial centres. It is true that, by way of compensation, the wages are lower, but the highly trained and thoroughly trustworthy working population, which we find in places given up exclusively to industry, is wanting. Instead of the increasing concentration of an industry into comparatively few works, the German cotton-spinning industry, even so recently as 1882,[2] with a total number of spindles amounting only to one-eighth of the English total, had, on the other hand, 6,751 establishments for cotton-spinning and weaving, as compared with 2,690 English ones. Of these 6,751, no less than

---

[1] Appendix R.

[2] For all the figures in the text relating to the situation of the German cotton industry, cf. "The Statistics of the German Empire," issued by the Imperial Statistical Office. New series. Vol. 6 (Berlin, 1886).

5,499 were still carried on at home. While in England, in 1885, each spinning or weaving mill had an average of 191 operatives, each spinning mill in Germany, in 1882, employed an average of 10 persons only, and in the same year there were still 5,977 persons severally engaged in spinning without machinery of any kind, and without assistance.

The technique of buying and selling is not less backward in Germany than is that of production. We find persons playing the part of employers whose command of capital by no means qualifies them to discharge that function, and who are compelled to have recourse to credit in a degree which threatens their existence at every fluctuation of the market. In connection with this, we find the division of labour among individual factories very imperfectly carried out. A machine-making industry, exclusively devoted to the special needs of the cotton industry, we find only in that part of Germany where that industry is also chiefly centred, namely, in Alsace. Of those improvements in the market which, as in England, do so much to cheapen raw material and to facilitate sale for the manufacturer, we find nothing beyond the first inadequate beginnings.

Nor do we suffer only from an excess of works belonging to an obsolete and inferior form of manufacture,—namely, that of home-industry,—but the technique of our large-scale factory industry is, on the average, also far behind the English. As against the average number of spindles per couple of English self-actors—namely, 2,000—we have only 1,300 to 1,600 in Germany. As is shown by the following table, the time taken by the inward and outward run of the self-actor is, in England, considerably smaller. According to the report issued by the German

Cotton Commission in 1878, the number of revolutions of the spindle in Germany is ten per cent. less than in England. Nevertheless, the German spindles have to stand idle during ten per cent. of the working day, as against the five per cent. only of the English spindles, owing to the inferior activity shown by the German workman in the joining of the broken threads. Moreover, the German spinning operative, with his less developed capacity of workmanlike production, makes high expenses of supervision necessary, which in England are wholly absent.

In the following table, Schulze-Gävernitz has summed up the comparison between the English and the German spinning mills.[1]

Expressed in words,[2] this amounts to the following :—

In England the workman looks after twice as much machinery as in Germany. The machines go faster. The losses in practice, as compared with the theoretical production of machines, are smaller. In regard to the last-named point it has to be considered that in England the taking off and putting on the reels takes less time, that the breakages of the thread are less frequent, and that the joining of the broken threads is done more quickly. The result is that the cost of labour per pound of yarn, especially if we include supervision, is decidedly smaller in England than in Germany. At the same time the wages of the English spinners are nearly twice as high as in Germany, and the working day little over nine hours as against eleven and eleven and a half in Germany.

It is the same in the weaving industry.

---

[1] Cf. Schulze-Gävernitz, "Grossbetrieb," pp. 138, 139.

[2] *Ibid.*, p. 135.

Locality.	No. of spindles per pair of self-actors.	No. of operatives. Spinners.	No. of operatives. Hel. pers.	Length of the outward run.	Duration in seconds of an outward and inward run.	Time worked per week in hours.	Week's output per pair of self-actors.	Spinner's wages in pfennig (10 pfennig = 1d.)	Spinner's weekly wage in marks. (1 mark = 1 shilling)	Average weekly wage of helpers in marks.	No. of spindles under one over-looker.	Weekly wage of the over-looker in marks.
1. 12's METRIC CHAIN				Metres			Kilogrammes	Per 1 Kilogramme				
Vosges	1272	2	3	1·6	13	66	1500	3·9	21	10·80	10000 to 20000	35—40
Mulhausen	1280	1	3	1·55	12·5	66	2050	3·15	24	13·50	,,	,,
2. 28's METRIC CHAIN												
Vosges	1272	2	3	1·6	15	66	900	8·89	21	10·90	,,	35—40
Mulhausen	1280	1	3	1·55	14	66	740	7·02	21	13·50	,,	,,
3. 20's ENGLISH TWIST				English inches			English lbs.	Per English lb.				
Bavaria	1568	1	3	64	15	65	2420	1·9 Pf.	18	10·70	15000	27
Württemberg	1200	1	4	65	15	65	1900	2·6 ,,	21	10·50	—	—
Saxony	2000	1	4	68	14	61	3600	1·7 ,,	22	11	10000	35
Oldham	2208	1	2	66	13	55	3432·5	1·8 ,,	45	15·25	—	—
4. 30's ENGLISH TWIST												
S. Germany	1672	1	3	63·8	16	65	1340	3·37 ,,	21	7·70	15000	20—30
Bolton	2004	1	2	64	14·6	55	2200	3·25 ,,	46	12·75	—	—
5. 36's ENGLISH TWIST												
S. Germany	1472	1	3	63·8	19	65	1055·5	4 ,,	21	7·70	15000	20—30
Switzerland	1200	1	2	65·9	17	65	850	3·9 ,,	18	7·50	11400	21·60
Saxony	1704	1	3	65·9	15	65	1550	3·35 ,,	21	8—13	5000	20—25
	2000	1	3	67	14	64	1900	3·2 ,,	22	9—13	10000	35
	2376	1	2	67	13	55	2182	3·25 ,,	38	17·75	—	—
Oldham	2688	1	3	67	13	55	2723·6	2·88 ,,	40·15	12·9	—	—
6. 40's ENGLISH TWIST												
Oldham	1560	1	3	65	13	55	1222	0·64	33s. 5d.	14s. 2½d.	—	—
Oldham	2400	1	2	64	13	55	1650	0·5d.	36s.	16s. 4d.	—	—
7. 60's ENGLISH TWIST												
Alsace	1248	1	3	60	22	69	530	9·75 Pf.	31 M.	12·50 M	12·15000	28·50
Bolton	1632	1	2	66	17·7	55	633·3	9·75 ,,	40 ,,	11 M.	—	—
8. 120's ENGLISH WEFT												
Alsace	1764	1	3	65	28	69	258	22·75 ,,	21·60 M	10·30 M.	8000	28·50
Bolton	2280	1	3	58	21	55	333·3	22·28 ,,	43 M.	11 M.	—	—

Here, too, we are encumbered with an endless number of individual home workers. The poor hand-loom weaver makes a martyr of himself in vain with his thirteen to sixteen hours day, and a weekly wage of three to seven shillings, in order to compete with the factory operatives working short hours for high pay. The effect of the frightful conditions under which he works on his efficiency is (I am speaking from official reports [1]), that he is too weak to undertake agricultural labour, and that he cannot even weave wider pieces of cloth without endangering his health.

But our inferiority is not confined to the hand-loom weavers. Even when it is a case of weaving by machinery, the German operative's efficiency in production is inferior to that of the Englishman to a degree corresponding to his inferior conditions of labour. As is shown by the following table, even in Alsace the number of picks of the loom per minute is thirty per cent. behind the English number.

Number of picks of the loom per minute in the weaving of plain cloth : [2]—

Width in Centimetres.	England.	Switzerland.	Alsace.
80–85	240	190–200	150–160
110–115	200	160–170	130–140
135–140	180	150–160	120–125
165–170	150	120–130	110–115

In addition to this, the loss in working the English weaving loom is ten per cent. less than in the case of the

---

[1] Appendix S.
[2] Schulze-Gävernitz, " Grossbetrieb," pp. 142, 143.

German. This explains the fact that in spite of a fifteen
per cent. shorter working day, the week's output in England is not smaller, but larger. But of course the English weaver's more intensive production is made possible
for him by wages which are nearly a third higher. The
following table [1] shows to what extent his production
surpasses that of the German operative :—

	Weekly production per weaver in yards.	Cost per yard.	Length of working day.	Weekly earnings of the operative.
Germany ...	466	0·303d.	12 hours	11s. 8d.
England ...	706	0·275d.	9 hours	16s. 3d.

These are results calculated to correct, not only the
traditional views, but also certain new ones which are
now struggling for the mastery.

In the first place there is the Social-democratic view
that the shortening of the working day will lead to
an absorption of the unemployed. This idea in its mechanical simplicity reminds one of the no less popular
idea, largely cherished by others besides Social-democrats,
that the advance in technical processes will diminish the
number of the men who are employed; and no doubt the
immediate effect of such advance is that "hands" do
become superfluous. But in 1760 the total number of
persons employed in the English cotton industry
amounted to 40,000 ; [2] in 1890 the number was 528,795 ; [3]
for in 1736 cotton yarn number 100 still cost £1 18s. per

---

[1] Schulze-Gävernitz, " Grossbetrieb," p. 151.

[2] Toynbee, " Lectures on the Industrial Revolution of England." London, 1884, p. 49.

[3] " Statistical Abstract," 1892, p. 179.

lb., while by 1832 it cost only 2s. 11d.,[1] and thereby
that great popular sale was won which has rendered it
possible to increase the number of the employed tenfold
and more. But not less erroneous than the notion that
the number of the unemployed is increased by advances in
technique is it to expect that the shortening of the working day will bring about the disappearance of the unemployed. In England the gradual shortening of the
working day since the beginning of factory legislation
has not led to a diminution of the unemployed; nor was
this the effect of the eight hours day in America and
Australia.[2] It is also obvious that it is not the length of
the working day of those employed that causes others to
be unemployed, and it is hard to see how a remedy which
leaves untouched the root of the evil can lead to its
removal. Lack of employment is due to the alternation
of ups and downs in the total economic life of the nation,
those workmen who were absorbed in the former period
being thrown on the streets again when the decline
comes round; another cause lies in the fluctuations in the
sale of articles produced for this or that season of the
year; and finally yet another in the too great popularity
of certain particular branches of industry and in the
demoralization of many workmen during the period of
decline due to those fluctuations. Now obviously all these
causes—the market fluctuations both in the total national
industry and in goods produced specially for this or that
season, not less than the economically irrational crowd-
ing into particular industries—remain just the same

---

[1] S. Porter, "Progress of the Nation." London, 1851. p. 181.
[2] Cf. John Rae, *Economic Journal*, i., p. 16 ff. Hadfield and
Gibbins, "A Shorter Working Day," pp. 92, 156, 160 ff.

after the shortening of the working day as they were before. It cannot therefore be expected from any such shortening of hours that it will prevent the dismissal of workmen in a time of diminishing demand.

Let us rather make use of what we have already learnt in order to enable ourselves to understand the effects of a short working day on the number of the employed. We have seen that in many cases the threatened decline of production was counterbalanced by the increased efficiency of the workman. In other cases it was neutralized by improved machinery or improvements in economic organization. In one way or the other, in most cases by the co-operation of both causes, *i.e.* greater efforts on the part both of workman and employer, instead of a decrease, an increase of production was effected. Only it is not every employer who can take active part in such advance. The narrow-minded and unenergetic manufacturer, with small capital and obsolete machinery, who at present just manages to hold his own with the help of wretched conditions of labour, will go under,[1] and we shall see his departure without tears. But all that means an increase and not a diminution in the number of the unemployed. Then no doubt a period of good trade once more appears and

---

[1] Cf. on this point the complaints in the memorandum of the Union of Austrian Cotton Spinners: "The new burden laid upon Austrian industry by the Eleven Hours Day" (Vienna, 1888). Similarly we read in the "Report on the Condition of Labour in Russia" (London, 1892, p. 8): "In Russia, the longer hours of labour are to be found in workshops of primitive construction and in those belonging to owners who are unacquainted, or pretend to be so, with modern developments of technique."

more workmen are wanted; but even if the then unemployed workmen of the different trades are thereby absorbed, yet the curtailment of the working day that has taken place does not prevent thousands from being once more thrown out of work when bad times come again.

It is true there are a number of occupations, such as the railway and the tramway services,[1] in which the shortening of the working day cannot be made good either by the increased efficiency of the workman or by improvements in the methods of working. In these cases the shortening of the working day would necessarily lead to the engagement of a proportionately larger number of workmen. Only it is very doubtful whether the unemployed workers of the other trades who have been as a rule demoralized during the previous periods of depression could be simply drafted into those unfamiliar occupations; for even employment on railways and tramways presupposes certain technical and moral qualifications.[2] Moreover, even granted that the railways and tramways may have absorbed at a given moment all the unemployed, this would not prevent the appearance of a new set of demoralized unemployed whenever depression in other industries once more set in.

On the one hand, therefore, the shortening of the working day by no means does away with the unemployed—it even, by leading to an increase of production,

---

[1] Cf. Sidney Webb and Harold Cox, "The Eight Hours Day," pp. 107, 129–134.

[2] Cf. Professor Munro, "The Probable Effects on Wages of a General Reduction in the Hours of Labour," in the Report of the sixtieth meeting of the British Association for the Advancement of Science. London, 1891, p. 473.

adds to the dangers of over-production; but, on the other hand, high wages and short hours cannot for their part limit the power of successful competition. And here we arrive at a point at which our conclusions come sharply into collision with certain received opinions.

If one reads the discussions before the conclusion of a treaty of commerce, in which the reduction of a customs duty is in question, one is regularly met, in Germany, by the argument that the lower wages and longer hours of Germany make it possible for her to compete with the more advanced England. The same argument is heard still oftener when any measure of social reform is the subject of debate. Nothing can be more perverse. "It is the long hours of foreign peoples which protect us from their competition," is the verdict of the President of the English Board of Trade, Mundella,[1] a man who was himself in his earlier years a partner in factories both in England and in Saxony. And as a matter of fact, high wages and short hours are a cause of England's advance, while it is the contrary that causes our backwardness; and the same holds good of our relations to America and to Australia.

Further, instead of that romantic preference for small master craftsmen and home industries which of late has begun to gain ground even among political economists, and instead of the dithyrambs to be found even in scientific works in honour of the admirable hand-loom weavers who are content with starvation wages of three to seven shillings a week,[2] just the opposite is what is

---

[1] Quoted by Hadfield and Gibbins, p. 127.
[2] Cf. Appendix S.

needed. Indeed, such romanticism is not merely to be
repudiated when it assumes an attitude of open hostility
to modern conditions, but also when it conceals itself behind the demonstration that the higher industrial systems
of working never quite supplant the older ones, but let
them live on, though it may be within certain narrower
limits ; for it is not here a question of the older systems
of working which have not been entirely supplanted,
but of the systems of working which stamp themselves
as antiquated by the fact that they are only kept
going by artificial protection both without and within.
The question is whether the most vital measures for
the elevation of the working classes, and whether the
interests of the great and growing industries which
would otherwise be victorious in the world's market, are
to be sacrificed to the interests of small masters and
producers who can neither live nor die. The continu-
ance of those petty businesses and home industries
which imply the acquiescence of those whom they
employ in the physiological minimum necessary to
support existence is, in fact, not only an obstacle in our
path whenever it is a case of obtaining reductions of
hostile tariffs by corresponding concessions in commercial
treaties, but also a direct cause of the limitation of our
competing power in the world's market.

And now it will not be hard to answer a further question which forces itself on the impartial observer.

How is it that it is not the countries which have the
most perfect factory legislation, the shortest working-
day, and the highest wages, that raise the cry that their
competing power is threatened, but those in which the
hours are longest and the wages lowest ?

The experience of all nations teaches us that it is just

those bad conditions of labour which they were anxious
to retain that have caused their backwardness. Those
conditions have acted like a prohibitive duty, checking
technical advance, while on the other hand high wages
and short hours have conduced the leading countries to
that advance which could only be attained with well-paid,
strenuous workmen, in other words with workmen whose
standard of living was a high one; and this applies to
all industries, not only to the textile ones. Schoenhof
shows us that the beam-hanger iron used in building,
for his labour at which the German smith is paid
3s., and the American 3 dollars per diem, is sold in
Germany at 9 cents, and in America at 3¾ cents a
pound.[1] He shows us how, in consequence of the use of
machinery, the labour which is paid 10 dollars 71 cents
in the Massachusetts clock-factories, is cheaper than the
labour paid 10 or 12 shillings at Trieberg in the Black
Forest.[2] To the European who congratulates himself on
Adam Smith's illustration of the advantages of division of
labour in the home industry of needle-making, by means
of which ten workmen daily produce 48,000 needles, he
shows a needle-factory in Connecticut where five workmen, by means of machines, daily turn out 7,500,000, in
the value of which the high wages paid to the workmen
are an element not worth considering. The experience,
that high wages are the cause of increased production,
holds good just as invariably for the different branches
of industry as for nations.[3]

Schoenhof is no less right in saying [4] that in the New
World it is only the fittest who survive in the struggle to

---

[1] Cf. Schoenhof, p. 98.   [2] *Ibid.*, p. 100.
[3] *Ibid.*, p. 99.   [4] *Ibid.*, p. 224.

exist; in the Old, it is hard to shake off the tenacious hold of the unfittest upon the industries in which they have once established themselves. For, in fact, low wages and long hours bring about a vicious circle from which, once one is within it, it is very hard to extricate oneself. For so long as labour is cheap, no technical progress seems necessary. It is bad labour conditions which are the main cause of the maintenance of inferior and long since antiquated methods. Then the employer appeals to the capital locked up in inferior processes of production and to the ruin with which he is threatened, in order to evade an improvement in the conditions of labour which would necessitate improved technique.

And yet, though hard, it is not impossible to break through this magic circle. All it requires is the courage to disregard the outcry of the unfit, and to follow the same policy in economic and social matters which we take for granted in the military domain. The battle is won so soon as we clearly understand that to attempt artificially to maintain antiquated systems of working and industries which cannot stand competition is a misguided romanticism, just as much as if we were to take the field with spear and shield against the serried artillery of the present, or to hold a picturesque mountain castle against melinite. We all know that, in war, that nation is victorious which can put into the field the most efficient soldier, armed with the best weapon, and we shrink from no sacrifice to secure for our country every possible progress in the military art. Just in the same way that relation of labour to cost of production which decides the victory in the world's market resolves itself entirely into

a question of equipment.[1] Whether labour is or is not
equipped with all improvements and inventions, whether
the workman is well maintained and fed, or under-paid
and over-worked—that decides the issue of the struggle.

The thought of those sacrifices for our military efficiency, which are imposed upon us by the geographical
position of our country, should act as a paramount inducement to us to create those conditions which alone
can bring us victory in the world's market. For it
certainly is not those economically unfit businesses
which can supply us either with the wealth or with
the men needful for the maintenance of our military
supremacy. They themselves exist only by the help of
artificial means, and at the cost of the healthy industries
of the country, and those who are employed in them are,
as we have seen, unequal to any kind of serious effort.

When, in 1806, the problem was to bring down-trodden
Prussia once more into the front rank, there was no
question of the classes, none of their having created the
Prussian State in the past and therefore of their having a
right to the special consideration of their interests in the
present. For the thought lay too close that the classes
which hitherto had held the decisive power in the State,
though they might have caused its greatness in the past,
had also been responsible for its collapse in the present.
Rather were men's efforts directed to break down the
wall of partition which divided the nobility from all other
classes. Instead of trying to maintain the previous
lords of the manor on their land, the privileged claim of
the nobility to the possession of such manorial lands was
set aside in order to put fit men in the place of the unfit.

---

[1] Cf. Schoenhof, p. 102.

On the same principle is to be explained the Edict of September 14th, 1811, which abolished the old prohibitions against the division of landed estates. On the same principle hereditary serfdom was abolished, and an effort made to regulate all forced services. On the same principle all trades were thrown open, all monopolies of sale at particular mills and inns were abolished, and "all props of idleness," as Hardenberg puts it,[1] done away. The guarantee for the new birth of the State was sought, not in the artificial protection of the economically unfit, but in the development of the powers of the fit. That policy has borne the most splendid fruits. But we have not yet ensured the permanency of what has been gained. Not until Germany has won the first economic place among the surrounding nations will she be in a position permanently to maintain the first political place which she now holds. And to this end we must have industries surpassing those of other countries, not only in a technical point of view, but in all that concerns the wages and efficiency of those whom they employ.

It is a joyful fact that the social reform which is to call up the millions to a higher stage of moral civilization, is also the sole means by which the economic and political supremacy of the nation can be permanently secured.

---

[1] Cf. Hardenberg's memorandum of 1807 on the reorganization of the Prussian State in Ranke's "Complete Works," vol. 48, pp. 361–414, and the Prussian economic legislation which thereon ensued.

APPENDICES.

A. (p. 5).

I HERE reprint the passage quoted by Adam Smith from the rare work of Messance. The title of the work is: "Recherches sur la Population des Généralités d' Auvergne, de Lyon, de Rouen et de quelques provinces et villes du royaume," par M. Messance, receveur des tailles de l'élection de St. Etienne, Paris, 1764. The passage referred to by Adam Smith (pp. 287–292 and 305–8) runs as follows :—

"It is not difficult to refute the supposed truth that the people only work when wheat is dear. No doubt there may be among the people artisans and day-labourers who, being naturally indifferent and indolent, cannot be spurred up to labour by anything but the extremest necessity, and who in years of plenty, when they are sure of their livelihood, do nothing for days or weeks; but this is far from being the universal behaviour of the people: artisans, day-labourers, and so on, do not work merely to earn a bare living, they want also to clothe themselves, their wives, and their children, and to procure the little comforts which their means permit them; and in practice we find that the years in which wheat is cheapest are those in which the people buy their furniture and their clothes. The proof is to be found in the industrial statistics of the Généralité of Rouen. Let the reader compare Tables iv., v., vi., vii. (at the end of this

Appendix), and he will find that in the years in which wheat was cheapest, the greatest mass of stuffs was produced. These statistics of the Généralité of Rouen are all the more remarkable and significant from the point of view of the question we are discussing, as all stuffs manufactured in it supply the demand of the people and the minor bourgeoisie, and accordingly belong to those very persons who would be most affected by the price of wheat. As the factories of the Généralité of Rouen were busiest in the years in which wheat was cheapest, it inevitably follows that the people worked more in those years, for the stuffs in question were produced only by workers who lived from hand to mouth. From the fact that the people were more fully occupied in the years of plenty than in the years of scarcity follows the impregnable demonstration,—first that the so-called maxim which asserts that the people are only induced to work by the extremest necessity is as false as it is unjust; second, that in years of plenty the people are in a position to consume more, to clothe themselves better, and to procure themselves the comforts of life, and that they are, so far, less unhappy; the Government is therefore a benefactor if it provides its people with their subsistence at the lowest possible price, and humanity alone must make all classes of society desire that the people may have the uninterrupted enjoyment of this precious benefit.

"M. de la Chalotai, advocate-general in the Parliament of Brittany, complains in the requisitorium which he drew up on the introduction of the edict of July, 1764, that day-wages, servants' wages, and all work and goods have, during the last century, notably advanced in price, although within the same period wheat has notably fallen; and he regards this as a loss to the State and an increase of the tax-payer's burdens. This official should, however, have observed that England, so notorious for her wealth, power,

and population, has experienced this very same alteration
in wheat prices on the one hand, and in prices of goods and
labour on the other. As the two kingdoms are in the same
position in regard to this important point, it is not easy to
exalt the felicity and power of the one, and to depreciate the
power and riches of the other, without falling into the most
obvious contradictions. That which Chalotai regards as a
misfortune is rather just that which constitutes the strength
of France, which widens the field of her commerce, and
has assured the greatest success to her industries. All
experts are of opinion that French commerce has made
surprising progress in the last forty years; that the branches
of industry pursued in the kingdom are far more fully
occupied to-day than they ever were before; that while our
old industries advance, a great number of new ones unknown
to our fathers have come into existence, and that it is just
the fall in the price of wheat, the necessary consequence of
which is the utmost possible consumption of industrial
products, to which these brilliant results are principally due.
Moreover, the advance of servants' wages, of day-wages, and
of the prices of goods, signifies a real advantage for the
needy part of the population, and brings them nearer to that
equality in the partition of the good things of life which
all modern philosophers apparently desire. Nor have the
landed proprietors in any degree lost thereby, for experience
shows that the rents of land have constantly risen, and there
is nothing extraordinary in that, as, on the one hand, the
increase of the population which we can observe in the
different provinces has increased the consumption of wheat,
and therefore brought new land under it. Plantations of
vines, apple trees, olive trees, and walnut trees have continually increased in the different parts of the country, and
supplied the landed proprietors with new sources of income,
and moreover the advance in manufacturing industry has led

G

to a marked increase of the cultivation of such raw materials
as flax, hemp, silk, rape-seed, weld and saffron, mulberry
trees, etc. On the other hand, the people whose position was
improved by the fall of the price of wheat have consumed
more wine and meat. This has favoured the breeding of
cattle, and has occasioned the breeding of a greater number ;
the consequence is : 1, that soils suited for vine-growing have
obtained a value which they formerly did not possess ; 2,
that meadow lands and other soils suitable for the rearing of
cattle have risen considerably in value ; 3, that the larger
number of cattle has led to a larger supply of manure, which
has made the ground more fertile, and that the harvests have
become more abundant. Finally, the improved condition of
the people has increased the consumption of wood alike for
building and for burning, and the proprietors of all these
different kinds of land have experienced an advance of
income. These different facts, which M. de la Chalotai has
undoubtedly overlooked, explain how it is that the landed
proprietors have lost nothing, although the price of wheat has
fallen, and servants' wages, day wages, and prices of manufactured good have risen. France is therefore in a happier
and more flourishing condition since the price of wheat has
fallen than it has been for eighty years. To raise the
price of the means of subsistence of her inhabitants would be
to deprive her of the greatest of her advantages. Considerations of humanity alone would make it, on the contrary,
desirable that the people should obtain their food more easily
and at less cost.

"It has been demonstrated that the low cost of wheat, far
from keeping the people from work, provides them with more
occupation and makes them more active and laborious. The
rich themselves are therein interested in consequence of the
certainty of their being able to obtain the manufactured
goods which they need more cheaply, for the price of all

such goods falls in proportion as consumption increases. As, however, this motive will not affect them so nearly as the apprehension of a fall in their rents, it is easy, by appealing to the strongest motive which can work upon the hearts of men,—namely, on the wish to preserve their life and health,—to show that they are as much interested in the lowest possible price of wheat as the poorest inhabitants of the country. For different statistical inquiries have, in fact, proved that in the years in which the price of wheat was highest, the mortality and the number of sick simultaneously attained their maximum, and *vice versâ* that in the cheapest years the mortality and the cases of illness were at their lowest. Such inquiries have taken place in Paris, London, Lyons, Rouen, and Clermont-Ferrand. The different tables which contain the results of these inquiries are printed below, and show quite unmistakably that the years of high prices are at the same time those of the greatest mortality and the most disease. The hospitals are, as the tables show, far fuller in the dear than in the cheap years. In the former, diseases are more dangerous, and it is impossible to prevent these diseases from attacking also the bourgeois, the well-to-do, the rich. The demonstration of all these truths will be seen to be irresistible if the reader will compare the results of the different tables with one another. The hospitals of Paris, Lyons, and Rouen almost uniformly show the same phenomena, and it is obvious that the mortality and the number of the sick are always in proportion to the price of wheat. The total of the deaths in Paris, London, and Clermont shows the same thing. Since, then, it has been proved that human life and health are largely dependent on the low price of wheat, that the years when it was low were invariably those in which there were fewest sick and dead, while on the other hand the years when it was high were those of the greatest mortality and disease, it

follows that all men, no matter of what rank and occupation
they may be, have an interest in getting the most necessary
means of subsistence at the lowest price, and that all landed
proprietors, landlords, and day-labourers should thank
Providence for a long series of fertile years, which by increase of production prolong their lives, protect them against
disease, provide them with the comforts which may miti-
gate the destitution in which the majority of them exist,
and finally, by means of the advance of manufacturing
industry, and the constant demand for its productions,
may provide them with a continuity of occupation which
is inseparable from the welfare of the State."

Of the tables which Messance prints in his appendix we
need here reproduce those only which are closely connected
with our subject, and are referred to by Adam Smith.

For the understanding of the following tables we should
add that, according to the wheat measures of Rouen, one
muid contained 12 septiers, 24 mines, 96 bushels. The
bushel was 143½⅜ per cent. smaller than the Berlin bushel.
The livre contained 20 sous, the sou 24 deniers. 81 livres=
80 frs. of present currency.

Table IV.

Comparison between the number of wool bales consumed
by the factory at Elbeuf, with the prices of corn from 1740
to 1763.

"The first column contains those years in which the
largest number of wool bales, the second those in which
the smallest number were sold. The number of wool bales
is taken from the octroi registry at Elbeuf. The price of
corn is reckoned according to the market rates at Easter,
Midsummer, Michaelmas, and Christmas."

Years.	No. of Wool Bales.	Price of a Quarter of Wheat on the Rouen Market.			Years.	No. of Wool Bales.	Price of a Quarter of Wheat on the Rouen Market.		
		Liv.	Sous.	Len.			Liv.	Sous.	Den.
1744	4753	6	11	9	1740	3802	18	0	0
1745	4477	6	13	9	1741	3672	17	11	9
1746	4521	8	1	3	1742	3903	9	15	0
1747	4897	10	0	0	1743	3727	7	3	9
1748	5137	10	7	6	1752	3190	13	15	0
1749	5830	10	12	6	1753	4258	13	7	6
1750	6127	10	7	6	1754	4393	10	10	0
1751	4842	12	10	0	1755	4381	9	7	6
1756	5080	8	18	9	1758	4008	12	15	0
1757	5307	15	15	0	1760	3370	12	1	3
1759	4589	10	16	3	1761	3968	9	10	0
1763	4997	8	15	0	1762	4461	9	15	0
Total	60507	119	9	3	Total	47133	143	11	9
Average	5042	9	19	1	Average	3927	11	19	3

TABLE V.

Comparison between the number of wool bales consumed in the Elbeuf factory, and the prices of corn from 1740 to 1763.

"Of these years the four have been chosen in which the largest number of bales was consumed,—they are given in the first column; in the second column of years are the four in which the smallest number was used."

Years.	No. of Wool Bales.	Price of the Quarter of Wheat (Rouen Measure).			Years.	No. of Wool Bales.	Price of the Quarter of Wheat (Rouen Measure).		
		Liv.	Sous.	Den.			Liv.	Sous.	Den.
1748	5137	10	7	6	1741	3672	17	11	9
1749	5830	10	12	6	1743	3727	7	3	9
1750	6127	10	7	6	1752	3190	13	15	0
1757	5307	15	15	0	1760	3370	12	1	3
Total	22401	47	2	6	Total	13959	50	11	9
Average	5600	11	15	7	Average	3490	12	12	11

TABLE VI.

Value of all sorts of cloths and silk stuffs examined and stamped, from 1744 to 1763, in the Inspector's Office of the Generality of Rouen.

"In the first column are those years in which manufacture was most active, in the second those in which it was least so."

Years.	Value of the Pieces.	Price of the Quarter of Wheat (Rouen Measure).			Years.	Value of the Pieces.	Price of the Quarter of Wheat (Rouen Measure.		
		Liv.	Sous.	Den.			Liv.	Sous.	Den.
1745	25,633,700	6	13	9	1744	22,528,666	6	11	9
1746	32,760,374	8	1	3	1751	24,923,077	12	10	0
1747	31,884,149	10	0	0	1752	24,855,512	13	15	0
1748	31.125,394	10	7	6	1756	24,869,528	8	18	9
1749	31,224,090	10	12	6	1757	24,996,656	15	15	0
1750	29,649,639	10	7	6	1758	20,779,987	12	15	0
1753	26,504,452	13	7	6	1759	19,867,080	10	16	3
1754	28,291,491	10	10	0	1760	20,318,768	12	1	3
1755	29,515,725	9	7	6	1761	23,486,882	9	10	0
1763	27,144,780	9	15	0	1762	24,916,387	9	15	0
Total	293,733,794	99	2	6	Total	231,542,543	112	8	0
Average	29,373,379	9	18	3	Average	23,154,254	11	1	9

TABLE VII.

Value of all sorts of cloths and silk stuffs examined and stamped, from 1744 to 1763, in the Inspector's Office of the Generality of Rouen.

"In the first column are the four years in which manufacture was most active, in the second the four in which it was least so."

Years.	Value of the Pieces.	Price of the Quarter of Wheat (Rouen Measure).			Years.	Value of the Pieces.	Price of the Quarter of Wheat (Rouen Measure).		
		Liv.	Sous.	Den.			Liv.	Sous.	Den.
1746	32,760,374	8	1	3	1744	22,528,666	6	11	9
1747	31,884,149	10	0	0	1758	20,779,987	12	15	0
1748	31,125,394	10	7	6	1759	19,867,080	10	16	3
1749	31,224,090	10	12	6	1760	20,318,768	12	1	3
Total	126,994,007	39	1	3	Total	83,494,501	42	14	3
Average	31,748,501	9	15	4	Average	20,873,625	10	11	1

B. (p. 6).

Cf. Arthur Young's "Travels" in France, in the years
1787–1790, Edition of 1792, p. 503. Speaking of French
manufactures he writes:—"Average earnings, in all the
fabrics, of the men, 26 sous; of the women, 15 sous; of the
spinners, 9 sous. These earnings are, without doubt, much
under those of similar manufactures in England; where I
should apprehend the men earn, upon an average, 20d.
a day, or 40 sous; the women 9d., or 18 sous; and
spinners I have shown ('Annals of Agriculture,' vol. ix.)
to earn 6½d., or 12½ sous. The vast superiority of English
manufactures, taken in the gross, to those of France, united
with this higher price of labour, is a subject of great
political curiosity and importance; for it shows clearly
that it is not the nominal cheapness of labour that favours
manufactures, which flourish most where labour is nominally
the dearest. Perhaps they flourish on this account, since
labour is generally *in reality* the cheapest where it is
nominally the dearest; the quality of the work, the skill
and dexterity of performance come largely into the account,
and these must on the average depend very much on the
state of ease in which the workman lives. If he be well

nourished and clothed, and his constitution kept in a state of vigour and activity, he will perform his work incomparably better than a man whose poverty allows but scanty nourishment."

C. (p. 12).

In the journal of the Royal Prussian Statistical Office, 1875, pp. 245–290. The *Concordia* (a manufacturer's journal on the labour question) of December 11th, 1875, also showed that Hiltrop's inquiries confirmed my views. It wrote as follows: "The output in 1873, when wages were higher, surpasses that of 1874 in no inconsiderable degree. In the former year it amounted to 197 tons per workman; in 1874 only to 183, or, including the nineteen new works, 187 tons; in particular the coal output in 1873 from 237 pits amounted to 16,439,831 tons, with 80,852 workmen, *i.e.* 203 per head; and in 1874 (241 pits) to 15,534,692 tons, with 80,530 workmen, *i.e.* 192 tons per man, and this, in spite of the fact that the number of shifts worked in 1874 was considerably larger than in 1873, and thus a 'greater regularity of work' already existed; notwithstanding, in that very year of 1873 the figures were 13·9 cwt. to the shift, while in 1874 they were only 13 cwt. (abstraction made of the nineteen new pits added in 1874), while in particular the coal mining of 1873 showed 14·3 cwt. to the shift, and that of 1874 only 13·3. It is no doubt merely a coincidence, but still noteworthy, that both wages and production fell almost exactly in the same proportion in 1874. Both, that is, fell about 7 per cent.; in the coalpits the average wage per shift in 1873 was 1 thaler, 7 silbergroschen, 4 pfennig, and in 1874, 1 thaler, 4 silbergroschen, 6 pfennig. The gain to the employers from the lowering of wages was consequently extremely unimportant. The latter is evident from a comparison of the total output with the total net wages in both years. These figures show that in 1873, five tons cost 8 thalers, 25 silbergroschen, 8 pfennig in wages; while in 1874 the wage-cost was 8 thalers, 23 silbergroschen, 7 pfennig (in the special case of coal-mining the figures were 8 thalers, 20 silbergroschen, 4 pfennig, and 8 thalers, 18 silbergroschen, 6 pfennig respectively); while if the production had in each case been the same, the difference would have amounted to about 15 silbergroschen, instead of to about two only."

D. (p. 15).

To enable the reader to test the equity of this un-favourable judgment, I here reprint those of Crowe's answers which bear upon the point.

They are to be found in the "First Report on the Depression of Trade and Industry," London, 1886, pp. 70, 71.

1076. (*Mr. Drummond.*) " Could you give us any idea, as the result of your observation with respect to the general position of the workmen on the Continent as compared with England, whether you think, making allowances for the difference in their mode of living, etc., they are as well off as English workmen?"—" I should say that they are not so well off."

1077. "Could you give us an idea as to their mode of working; do you think that they work as hard as English workmen do?"—"Certainly not."

1078. "Notwithstanding the increased number of hours worked on the Continent, the amount produced would not be so great as in England?"—"No; that is so."

1079. (*Earl of Dunraven.*) "In all industries?"—"Yes, in all industries."

1082. (*Sir J. P. Corry.*) "You told us, also, that in Germany the facilities for producing cheap goods were greater than in England; in what way is that so?"- "The wages are lower."

1083. "Are there any other matters that require to be brought into consideration?"—"I think that is a very potent factor. The same factor which works in Belgium enables the Belgians to beat, not only the French, but the Germans and ourselves. As you perhaps know as well as I, girders were sold the other day at Barnsley which were imported from Belgium."

1084. (*Earl of Dunraven.*) " Is it your opinion that that is owing entirely or partly to the wages? "—" Partly owing to cheaper wages, and partly owing to that system which I spoke of, which is in force in Germany, that is, that the export tariff for carrying is cheaper, and made cheaper for the purpose of these things. Possibly, also, there may have been some reason in the form of those girders which were patented."

1085. (*Sir J. P. Corry.*) " You just told us a moment ago that although the wages are lower and the hours longer, the men do not work as hard on the Continent as they do in England? "—" That is quite so."

1086. " Does not the one balance the other? "—" No, it does not."

1087. " In what way? "—" *Ceteris paribus*, you must have cheap wages to get over the whole of the elements which cause the difference. If, all the other factors being equal, the wages were lower in Germany than in England, it would be a simple sum in arithmetic. The wages are cheaper, but they must be cheaper still under the other form to compensate at the same time somewhat for the greater idleness of the working hands."

1088. " What I want to get to is this: do those longer hours and lower wages that exist on the Continent compensate for the greater amount of work that is got out in England? "—" There would be in each case a calculation to make; the question of cheaper work overrules all the other points, I should think."

1089. (*Earl of Dunraven.*) " I suppose you have not made any calculation on that point? "—" No; it would be very difficult to make any general calculation."

1115. (*Mr. Drummond.*) "We have been continually told that work has been sent to the Continent because of the lowness of wages and the greater number of hours worked. I understand from your evidence now that the amount of work produced per day is admittedly considerably less than that produced by Englishmen in the same period, and that the one, to a great extent, counterbalances the other. Are we really to understand that, because, if so, it upsets the idea altogether as to work being driven out of the country on account of the difference in wages and hours?"—"I was saying just now that it is a very difficult thing to measure the exact failing quantity in the daily labour of a workman; that is to say, the difference between what one workman in Germany does in so many hours, and what an English workman does in so many hours. The question, however, is not so simple. As I said before, you cannot pit the one against the other, you must take into account other factors, and these are difficult to get. But I held, and I still hold, to this, that although the German workman produces less in a day than an English workman, and works cheaper, the action of the cheaper working is the dominant factor in the calculation."

1116. (*Mr. Aird.*) "There are two differences: one, the the question of time, they work so much longer than here, that is one point; and there is another point, namely, that they receive so much less wages there than they do here?"—"Yes, that is the case."

1117. "And if I may be allowed to suggest, what I think you meant was, that as regards the question of time, an English workman in a shorter time will do as much work as a foreign workman in a longer time; but you have still the difficulty of the difference of wages to overcome."—"Precisely so."

1118. (*Mr. Drummond.*) "I think the position is this, and that your own observation will confirm it: a French workman, for example, seems to us to go about his work in a lackadaisical fashion rather than otherwise; in many cases there seems to be less supervision exercised than in England, is that so?"—"No doubt that is so; they are more leisurely in their mode of working; but I cannot come to the conclusion that because it is so, therefore the balance is restored."

1124. "(*Mr. A. O'Connor.*) But still you are decidedly of opinion that although the average efficiency of the German workman is not so high as the average efficiency of the British workman, the cost of production in Germany on the whole is less than the cost of production in Great Britain? —Yes, I should say so."

E. (p. 15).

In view of the importance of Bell's statements, I think it well to give here verbatim the contents of that part of the "Statement relating to the Iron Trade of the United Kingdom," prepared by Sir Lowthian Bell, Bart., Fellow of the Royal Society. It is to be found in the "Second Report on the Depression of Trade and Industry," London, 1886, pp. 340–345.

"The power of producing cheaply depends on the cost and efficiency of human labour. This remark applies with great force to an article like iron, in which, with the exception of the royalties and profit on railway carriage, the expense of manufacture consists almost entirely in wages paid to workmen. Every one who has had any experience in the work performed by his men, knows, as might be expected, how close the connexion is between efficient labour and food, which latter ought to be cheap and good. In former days, when low-priced labour abroad was spoken of, its cost was generally attempted to be explained by the low character of the nourishment upon which the workmen there were content to subsist. This is a mistake; badly fed men are never good workers; but this fact does not affect the

proposition respecting the importance of cheap food, provided it is of proper quality.

"My own observations while on the Continent agree with
those of all writers on the gradual rise in the cost of provisions there during the last thirty years and more. This
may be partly accounted for by the increase of population,
by the introduction of new branches of industry, and, lastly,
by our free trade policy in this country, which, aided by
improved modes of transport, has enabled us to reap part of
the advantages flowing from the fertile soils of France,
Germany and other countries.

"A French coal-owner gave me the result of his own personal experience which I repeat as he told it. The figures
are in French weights and currency, and apply to every
tenth year.

TABLE XXXV.

	1830.	1840.	1850.	1860.	1870.	1878.	Increase from 1830 to 1878.
	fr.	fr.	fr.	fr.	fr.	fr.	Per cent.
Butcher's meat per kilo	0·62	·75	1·01	1·06	1·34	1·66	167
Butter per kilo	1·50	1·55	1·74	1·86	2·57	3·04	102
Potatoes per hectolitre	2·33	3·12	4·31	4·25	4·06	4·82	107
Shoes per pair	2·45	2·17	2·50	3·24	4·68	6·53	166
Coarse cloth per metre	4·16	8·05	7·56	8·20	7·68	7·12	71

"I could multiply proofs to the same effect almost without
end, from Germany and elsewhere, obtained by myself and
observed by others, but that will probably be considered need-
less. I may remark, however, that the purchasing power of
money in reference to provisions was never more favourable
in Great Britain than it is now. Seeing that we are bringing
from America and India together about as much wheat as
we grow ourselves, besides other articles of domestic con-

sumption, at a low rate of freight and unhampered with import duty, and that other European nations are also importers, paying a little more for freight and often a duty besides, it is an indication that Great Britain is probably as well circumstanced as its neighbours in respect to the means of feeding its people.

"With the increased cost of the means of subsistence abroad, it is not surprising that foreign workmen should have demanded higher wages. In 1827 coal-hewers could be had in France for 1s. 5½d. per day; in 1869 their pay had risen to 3s. 1¾d., and in the excitement of 1873 and 1874 it reached 3s. 9½d. per day.

"The following figures, taken from the experience of a French colliery owner, illustrate the connexion (one, however, that the English coal-owner did not experience in 1873) between better pay and improved efficiency."

	1860.	1869.	1872.	1873.	1874.	1875.	1876.
	s. d.	s. d.	s. d.	s. d.	s. d.	s. d.	s. d.
Coal hewer's wages per week	10 7½	12 8¾	15 7½	17 2	16 1½	15 4¾	16 1¼
Cwt. of coal worked per man per day	41·53	61·20	68·82	67·6	60	60	58·46

In reproducing this table Sir Lowthian Bell remarks that in 1873 the English colliery owner might well fail to perceive the connexion between higher wage and higher production. But as the table shows, in that year such a connexion is equally wanting in France, and not less so (so far as that year is concerned) in the Belgian figures quoted by Sir Lowthian Bell later on. The reason is a very simple one, and was clearly explained on the occasion of the arbitration in the wages dispute between the Northumbrian colliers and the mine owners in 1875. (Cf. "Schriften des Vereins für Socialpolitik," vol. 45, p. 146.—Rupert Kettle's judgment as Arbitrator). During the feverish boom in the trade that followed the close of the Franco-German war, on the one hand a number of less productive seams were worked, while on the other hand the working staff was enlarged by a considerable number of unskilled workmen. The consequence was on the one hand a proportionately smaller total output, and on the other hand a larger divisor, and therefore, when the average production per head of the working staff was calculated, a smaller output per individual workman.

The same mistake, namely the failure to allow for the greater or less natural productivity of the seams, is perpetrated by Sir Lowthian Bell when he goes on to compare the production and the wages of the workmen in the different German coal-districts, as well as the wages and production of the colliers in the different nations. The figures advanced are quite worthless. Thus, for instance, when he writes :—

" Dealing with the mining class generally (coal and iron-stone) in the North-Eastern district of England, and *disregarding any differences in the facility of extraction of the minerals themselves*, I have estimated that their comparative cost of labour is approximately represented by the following numbers :—

England.	Germany.	Belgium.	France.
100	95	124	103."

How little value Sir Lowthian Bell himself attaches to these figures is shown by the fact that he writes, in direct opposition to the above, " It is my firm conviction that the greater production of the English collier is mainly due to his better pay and his higher standard of living." The statements of the Northumberland coal-owners before the Court of Arbitration in 1875 are in complete harmony with this latter view. (Cf. " Schriften des Vereins für Social-politik," vol. 45, pp. 47 foll.)

Not less dubious appears to be the value of Sir

Lowthian Bell's reference to an unnamed German authority, whose view was that the Continent perhaps derived
from its lower wages an advantage over England in
those industries in which skilled labour preponderated,
so that muscular power mattered less than skill, as for
instance in the production of steam-engines and compli-
cated machinery. For, it is quite obvious from the nature
of Sir Lowthian's reference, that the view of the unnamed
German authority is founded only upon a conjecture and not
upon observation and calculation. Moreover, even if we
were to assume that the latter was the case, even so, simply
to contrast the production of low-paid skilled German
labour with that of high-paid skilled English labour,
would be insufficient for our question unless at the same
time we took into account the much higher degree in which
in Germany the cost of producing the skilled workman is
defrayed from public resources. For it is clear that where,
as in Germany, a far higher proportion of the cost of training
the skilled workman is met from public funds, the pay of
the workman can be lower, and that even with a lower
wage higher production can be attained than in cases where
the wage alone has to replace the total costs of training. If
therefore we are considering the question how far the rate
of wages influences the capacity of production in those
branches of industry which are conducted in the main with
skilled labour, we must allow ourselves to contrast such cases
only as resemble each other so far as the method of defraying
the cost of training is concerned. Schoenhof has done this,
and the evidence given in the text demonstrates that skilled
labour is no exception to the rule, but that, in its case also,
higher wages are the condition of higher capacity of production.

I pass over the further statements of Sir Lowthian Bell
about the cost of labour in shipbuilding, as they rest in
part on unverifiable newspaper reports, in part are obscure,

while they are contradicted by the statements of one of the greatest English shipbuilders referred to later on.[1] On the other hand, there is no doubt that his own personal observations concerning the cost of labour in the iron industry deserve the closest attention.

"In the year 1879 I obtained from the different works statements of the daily earnings paid to what may be considered the skilled men in a plate mill. The following is the result of my inquiries:—

	German Works.		English Works.	
	s.	*d.*	*s.*	*d.*
Head puddler	5	8	6	1
Second puddler	5	3½	3	6
Third puddler	4	0	none	
Boy puddler...	1	7½	none	
Puddle roller	5	1¾	15	1
Shingler	5	3	22	9
Furnace men at plate mill	6	6¼	16	1
Plate rollers, average of five men	4	6¼	Head roller 41	1
Head shearers, average of eight men ··· ...	5	3½	Head shearer 31	9

"The enormous differences exhibited by these figures must not be accepted as the actual excess of cost in England as compared with Germany; firstly, because in certain branches of labour, such as engine-men, labourers, etc., the discrepancy is less in amount than in the case of the instances given above; and, secondly, the number of men employed is often larger abroad than with us.

"I have endeavoured to compare the actual cost on a given amount of work, and below is given the result of my estimates:—

---

[1] Appendix J.

H

	Ger- many.	Eng- land.		Ger- many.	Eng- land.
PUDDLING MILL.	£	£	FINISHING MILL.	£	£
Delivering materials	4·42	2·45	Delivering materials	2·13	5·34
Engine and firemen	3·30	8·30	Enginemen and fire-		
Puddlers	63·25	108·50	men	4·80	5·00
Shinglers	4·50	11·10	Furnace men . . .	16·40	30·66
Bogey men, rollers,			Piling iron, rollers		
etc.	22·64	12·10	and shearmen . .	74·03	60·50
Sundry labour . .	1·89	2·55	Sundry labour . .	2·64	8·50
	100·00	145·00		100·000	110·00

Let us next take Sir Lowthian Bell's statements about the labour-cost in the Bessemer process in the two countries respectively:—

"Returns were made in 1879 and 1880 from English and German works, which showed that in the former, at the converting department, the rates varied from 4s. 6¾d. to 7s. 0½d. per day, the average on the whole being 6s. 2¼d., whereas in the latter the prices paid ran from 2s. 0¼d. to 2s. 11½d., the average being 2s. 8d.

"In the English rail mill the lowest wages paid were 3s. 2¼d. and the highest 23s. 2d., per day, against 2s. 6d. and 8s. 7d. in the German mill. The average earnings in the former being 5s. 3¾d., and 3s. 3d. per diem in the latter.

"On comparing the relative amount of work done in each case the relation between the two is estimated to be as follows:—

	Eng- land.	Ger- many.
CONVERTERS.		
Work performed per man, England taken as unity	100	81·17
Cost of labour on ingots	100	63·24
Average daily earnings	100	43·24
RAIL MILL.		
Work performed per man	100	100·00
Cost of labour per ton of rails	100	86·11
Average daily earnings	100	61·18

" These figures show a considerable advantage in favour of the German mill, which on the finished article may be taken to amount to a difference of 24 per cent. All this, however, and perhaps more, will be absorbed in the expense of placing the rails on board a ship for exportation."

At the conclusion of the passage in question, Sir Lowthian Bell writes:—

" To some extent the cost of labour on the ton of iron may be accepted as an index of the general fitness of the establishment for the work done. Judged by this criterion, partly owing to the excellence of the arrangements for avoiding human agency, and partly owing to the geographical position of the raw materials, I have seen no smelting works in the old world or new which could compare with the Middlesborough practice. If those in any foreign country are equal, I will not say superior to it, a change must have been effected since my visits, and since I have received foreign visitors who all remark on the comparatively fewer hands employed at Middlesborough than in their own country. To some extent this has to be attributed to the efficiency of our better fed men, a fact which I have heard generally admitted abroad."

Since Sir Lowthian Bell presented his report on December 16th, 1885, the American iron industry has outstripped the English for the very same reasons which have enabled the latter to surpass all the other iron-industries of the world, namely, better fed workmen and highly developed arrangements for economising human labour.

F. (p. 16).

Report of the Iron Inquiry Commission to the Federal Council (Session of 1878-1879). No. 24, p. 36. " The reports on the cost of production at home and abroad, and the comparison of such cost with present prices, confirm the decline of the economic position of the iron industry. This decline is also confirmed by statistics, according to which the value of 2,240,574 tons of pig-iron produced in 1873 amounted to £12,430,738, while that of the 1,934,725 tons produced in 1877 amounted to £5,582,668, and in the same way the 1,583,986 tons of malleable and fused iron produced in 1873 were valued at £21,919,382, while the 1,503,052 tons of similar material produced in 1877 were valued at £12,177,032. (pp. 34 and 35).

"The reaction of this fall in the price of iron upon the condition of the workmen lies in the nature of the circumstances.

"It is clear from the figures given, that the number of workmen employed in the iron industry proper has diminished, and that in a higher degree than might have been expected from the fact that the iron produced has been almost identical in quality since 1871.

"By way of explanation we have been told that the production of the workman has increased both in itself and by improvements in the technical processes.

"The rates of wages prevailing in 1869 rose in the course of a few years—up to 1873—as much as 30 and 40 per cent., and even doubled in certain branches, but have again gone back with few exceptions to the standard of .1869.

"In view of the rise in price of all the necessities of life which has since come about, and in view of the greater demand made upon the tax-paying power of the workmen, whose contribution to public purposes is, in some communities, reckoned at 3 to 5 per cent. of their total earnings, the further lowering of wages with a view to diminishing the cost of production is unanimously regarded as inadmissible if the working power of the labourers is not to be diminished, and their physical and moral welfare is not to be endangered.

"Though the assertion has been made on many sides that the sudden rise in wages, consequent upon the heavy demands made upon the iron industry in 1871 and 1872, exercised in many cases an unfavourable influence upon the working population, so that the result of labour was thereby frequently lowered both in quantity and in quality, nevertheless it has been demonstrated that every rise in wages justified by the circumstances has had a favourable effect on the working population both as regards their efficiency and their morality.

"The concurrent opinion of experts that the production of English and Belgian workmen and, in some points also, of the Frenchmen must be rated higher than that of the Germans, appears to us to be of great importance."

G. (p. 27).

It seems all the more unjust to direct this charge exclusively against Senior, as Senior himself (at the Social Science Congress at Edinburgh, in 1863) gave the following explanation, which is not very remote from Marshall's own views :—

"The sciences of which the operations of the human mind are the principal subject derive their premises principally from consciousness. Such a science is Political Economy. The operations of the human mind, in producing, accumulating, buying and selling, form nine-tenths of its premises. If all men's minds were similar, those premises would be based solely on consciousness. As men's minds differ in detail, though generally similar in their great features, a teacher of Political Economy may sometimes find that in appealing to the consciousness of his pupils, he is arguing on a false premise, the identity of his pupils' consciousness and his own. He is forced, therefore, sometimes to correct his consciousness by observation, and to admit that the conduct, which, if he judged from his own feelings, he would describe as universal, is in fact only general. To this source of error men of the highest genius are peculiarly subject. As their minds are, by the supposition, peculiar, when they judge of others by themselves, they must sometimes judge falsely.

"Mr. John Stuart Mill has proposed to escape from this difficulty in Political Economy, by treating that science hypothetically, by defining man as a creature employed solely in the production and accumulation of wealth, and by then explaining how such a being would act and feel. Political Economy so treated would be strict science; as strict as that of Logic. Its premises would all rest on consciousness and on definitions; and its conclusions, unless illogical or tinctured by the teacher's peculiarities, could not be denied. As Mr. Mill has not adopted this hypothesis in his great work, I presume that he found on experience that such a treatment of his subject would, from its want of reality and of practical application, be uninteresting."

H. (p. 27).

Cf. The Edinburgh Review, vol. 83 (1846), p. 88; also several passages in *The Westminster Review*. In vol. 49 (1848), for instance, which I happen to have at hand, it is urged against Lord Ashley's Ten Hours Act, which limited the hours of the women and children working in the textile factories, "That it is the competition of workmen among themselves that regulates the hours of labour, and not the good pleasure of the masters or the will of a legislature. True, a factory may be closed at six in the evening, or shut up altogether if it so please a government; but what law can prevent the hand-loom weaver, who is his own master, working eighteen hours out of the twenty-four, when the power-loom is idle? (and this is a common case)." Thus the academic Quarterlies. In the newspapers, on the other hand, which were the organs of the economists of the

day, such as the *Examiner*, Lord Ashley and his followers
were stigmatised with the name of Jack Cade, the leader of
the peasant revolt (*cf.* "Greville Memoirs," second part, ii.,
p. 237). It was this attitude of the economists of the day
which led Fielden to give a supplementary title to his
pamphlet in favour of the Ten Hours Act, quoted on p. 22.
It was entitled "The Curse of the Factory System; or, the
Folly of the Political Economists."

I. (p. 31).

As it is often said that the English cotton industry has
of late declined, and in order that further false conclusions
may not be drawn from this mistaken notion, I here reproduce the tables compiled by a distinguished expert, Elijah
Helm, in the *Economic Journal* for December, 1892:—

CONSUMPTION OF RAW COTTON IN THE UNITED KINGDOM.

	Bales of 400 lbs. each.	Years.	Bales of 400 lbs. each.
1873-74	3,165,320	1886-87	3,694,000
1877-78	2,941,120	1887-88	3,841,000
1882-83	3,744,000	1888-99	3,770,000
1883-84	3,666,000	1889-90	4,034,000
1884-85	4,433,000	1890-91	4,230,000
1885-86	3,628,000	1891-92	3,977,000

The consumption in 1873-74 was thus very large, and yet
it is exceeded by that of 1891-92, to the extent of 24 per
cent.

The following table shows an increase in the export of yarn
from 1874 to 1891, to the extent of 11·1 per cent., in that of
cloth to the extent of 36·2 per cent. Moreover, in considering
the statistics of the export of yarn, it should be borne in mind
that yarn for exportation has become finer, which explains

EXPORTS OF COTTON YARNS AND PIECE-GOODS.

Years.	Yarns.	Value per lb.	Piece Goods.	Plain Cloths, value per yard.
	lbs.	d.	yards.	d.
1874	220,682,919	15·79	3,606,639,044	3·22
1878	250,631,800	12·17	3,618,655,300	2·76
1883	264,772,000	12·25	4,538,888,500	2·61
1884	270,904,600	12·24	4,417,280,000	2·47
1885	245,809,900	11·58	4,374,516,500	2·33
1886	254,331,100	10·84	4,850,210,000	2·21
1887	251,026,000	10·88	4,904,012,000	2·27
1888	255,846,100	10·94	5,038,307,000	2·27
1889	252,435,800	11·13	5,001,239,100	2·24
1890	258,290,800	11·47	5,124,966,000	2·30
1891	245,258,700	10·94	4,912,475,700	2·31
1892*	195,048,700	—	4,031,271,000	—

the proportionately small increase in the weight of the exported yarn compared with the export of cloth.

It should be added that during the same time the consumption of cotton in England itself rose from 244,000,000 lbs. in 1883, to 319,937,000 lbs. in 1891.

J. (p. 32).

John Scott, shipbuilder at Greenwich, on April 8th, 1886, gave the following answers before the Royal Commission on the Depression of Trade and Industry (Third Report, p. 189):

"11933. You formerly had a shipbuilding establishment in France, had you not?—Yes; twenty years ago I had considerable experience of that.

"11934. In your experience, did you find a very great difference in the amount of labour that a Frenchman turned out in a day compared with the amount that a Scotchman turned out?—Some of the classes of workmen in France I

---

* To end of October.

found did most excellent work. The shipwrights, I think, will compare with any shipwrights here. I found them working too long hours.

"11935. What hours were they working when you first went there? Twelve hours a day. I reduced that to ten hours, and found that it was advantageous, so far as I was concerned."

K. (p. 36).

Sidney Webb and Harold Cox, authors of "The Eight Hours' Day," put questions to those firms which had introduced the eight hours' day, with regard to its effects: (1) on the amount of the weekly production; (2) on the cost of production; (3) on the extent of overtime; (4) on the workman's wages paid by time; (5) on his wages paid by piece-work; and (6) on the relations between employers and employed. The queries were sent to the Chemical Works of Messrs. Burroughs, Wellcome & Co., London; to the Alkali and Soda Works of Brunner, Mond & Co., Northwich; to the Type Foundry of Caslon & Co., Chiswell Street, London, E.C.; to the Machine Works of S. H. Johnson & Co., Stratford, London, E.; to the Printers and Engravers, Green, MacAllen & Fielding, London; to the Book Printing Works of the *Star* newspaper, London; to Mark Beaufoy, M.P., manufacturer of vinegar and British wines and preserves; and to the Municipality of Huddersfield, with regard to their tramways. The replies received were satisfactory from every point of view, with the exception of the experiments made by the firm Green, MacAllen & Fielding, who pay their people by time, and who declared themselves in favour of a legal eight hours' day, because otherwise they would be unable to compete with the firms working longer hours. It is clear from their letter that the firm made the experiment in the hope of getting the custom of the workmen's organizations, and that hope being disappointed, they returned to the nine hours. See Webb & Cox, pp. 255-264.

Messrs. R. A. Hadfield and H. de B. Gibbins, authors of " A Shorter Working Day " (Methuen & Co., London, 1892), have made similar collections of facts, showing equally good results.

The first of the two authors, Hadfield, is proprietor of the Hadfield Steel Foundry at Sheffield. He first reduced the working day in his works from nine to eight and a half hours, with favourable results. No less successful than the experiments quoted by Webb & Cox was that of Short Brothers, shipbuilders in Sunderland. *Cf.* Hadfield & Gibbins, *op. cit.*, pp. 135-153.

L. (p. 37).

Cf. The Right Hon. J. Chamberlain, M.P., " The Labour Question," in the *Nineteenth Century* for Nov., 1892. Earlier in the same year (March 23rd, 1892), in the parliamentary debate on the Miners' Eight Hours' Day, Chamberlain made the following statements: " When I was in business—I am speaking of twenty years ago—my firm were working under great pressure, twelve hours a day. Shortly afterwards the Factory Acts were applied to Birmingham, and we reduced the hours to ten a day. Some time later we voluntarily reduced the hours to nine a day, after the experiment at Newcastle of a nine hours engineers' day. We were working self-acting machinery. All the workmen had to do was to feed the machines and see the tools were kept in order. In this case, if in any, the production should be directly proportionate to the number of hours worked. What is the fact? When we reduced the hours from twelve to ten—a reduction of 17 per cent.—the reduction in the production was about 8 per cent. When we again reduced the hours from ten to nine—a reduction of 10 per cent.—the reduction of production was 5 per cent."

M. (p. 37).

The agreement drawn up between the Central Union of London Building Contractors and the representatives of the London Building Workmen, so far as it relates to hours of labour, runs as follows :—

1. The working hours in summer are to be 50 hours per week, on the first 5 week days from 6.30 to 8, from 8.30 to 12, and from 1 to 5; on Saturdays, from 6.30 to 8, and from 8.30 to 12.

2. During 14 weeks in the winter, from the first Monday in November, the working hours are to be $8\frac{1}{2}$ hours daily for the first 3 weeks, 8 hours during the 8 intermediate weeks, and during the 3 following weeks $8\frac{1}{2}$ hours, the 8 hours being thus divided—on the first 5 week days 7 to 8, 8.30 to 12, and 12.30 to 4. During the first three and last three weeks of winter, 4.30 p.m. is to be the hour for leaving work. On Saturdays, hours to be from 7 to 8, and from 8.30 to 12.

Whence it follows that the working hours are fixed at 50, excepting for 6 weeks in the year, during which they amount to 47, and 8 during which they amount to $44\frac{1}{2}$ hours only, an average of $48\frac{21}{28}$ per week.

Wages at the same time to be raised a halfpenny an hour. Overtime to be worked only at the special request of the contractor, and to be paid according to its duration, at $1\frac{1}{4}$, $1\frac{1}{2}$, or twice the ordinary rate.

N. (p. 46).

Cf. also Werner von Siemens, "Lebenserinnerungen," p. 216 (Berlin, 1892). Siemens started a copper foundry at Kedabeg in the Caucasus, which is now in full activity. The whole neighbourhood has been civilized by his enterprise. Neat workmen's dwellings have taken the place of wretched clay hovels. On the introduction of these dwellings, Siemens writes in full accord with the statement of the text: "It gave the mining managers at Kedabeg a great deal of trouble to accustom their Asiatic workmen to stone houses. When, with the help of their wives, this object was finally attained, the difficult labour question was therewith also solved. The wants of the people of that country being extremely few, they have no inducements to work much. As soon as they have earned enough money to live on for a few weeks, they stop working and take their ease. The only remedy for such a state of things was to habituate them to wants which could only be satisfied by continuous labour." Siemens goes on to describe how a sense for a higher standard of comfort first awoke in the women and gave them higher wants, for the satisfaction of which their husbands had to provide, "while the latter themselves found by experience the benefit," and how, in the end, there was a general rush for the workmen's dwellings. In that way the natives who, owing to the absence of wants, had hitherto been content with their cave-dwellers' existence, and needing nothing, had worked as little as possible, were induced to steady labour. "I can only strongly recommend a similar course of action in the case of our present colonial enterprises. The man without wants is an enemy to every development in civilization. It is only when wants have been awakened in him, and he has become accustomed to labour for their satisfaction, that efforts to civilize him in the social and religious sphere have any prospect of success. To begin with such efforts will never produce any but illusory results."

O. (p. 59).

The following account of the causes of this transference is given by Elijah Helm (*Economic Journal*, ii. 738), in agreement with the view taken by the text:—

"Among the chief reasons for this transference of cotton spinning from North to South Lancashire are: (1) the fact

that in the latter the system of building gigantic mills,
worked—because of their magnitude and their structural
improvements—at greatly reduced cost, was first established;
(2) that this movement was encouraged by the close
proximity of the foremost spinning-machine making works
in the world by the concurrent growth in and around
Oldham of a superior class of spinning workpeople, and by
the founding of a local share market, and of a body of men
who found profitable employment in the formation of new
spinning companies. Perhaps also the comparative nearness
of Oldham to Liverpool, the great cotton depôt, and to
Manchester, the great yarn market, may be named as an
auxiliary cause. Meanwhile, it was not only the absence of
these circumstances in the northern half of the county
which brought about the decay of spinning there. The older
mills, once prosperous, were either too small, or were con-
structed upon abandoned plans, ill adapted, or incapable of
adaptation to modern methods," etc.

P. (p. 61).

Elijah Helm (*Economic Journal*, ii. 737) gives the following table of the number of cotton spindles in the United
Kingdom and the average consumption of cotton per spindle
in lbs. :—

Years.	Spindles.	Consumption per Spindle.
1874	37,515,772	33·7
1878	39,527,920	30·0
1883	42,000,000	35·0
1884	43,000,000	34·0
1885	43,000,000	32·0
1886	42,700,000	34·0
1887	42,740,000	34·0
1888	43,500,000	35·0
1889	43,500,000	34·0
1890	43,750,000	37·0
1891	44,750,000	38·0
1892 ?		

Q. (p. 61.)

The "Statistical Abstract" for 1892 (p. 179) gives the following table of employment in the cotton mills:—

Number of persons employed—

Years.	Males.				Females.			Total No. of Males and Females.
	Age.			Total No. of Males.	Age.		Total No. of Females.	
	Under 13.	From 13 to 18	Over 18.		Under 13.	Over 13.		
1870	23,142	38,209	117,046	178,397	20,139	251,551	271,690	450,087
1874	33,672	38,557	115,391	187,620	33,228	258,667	291,895	479,515
1878	28,663	34,730	122,079	185,472	33,260	264,171	297,431	482,903
1885	23,904	40,205	132,269	196,378	26,088	281,603	307,691	504,069
1890	22,701	43,561	149,925	208,187	25,432	295,176	320,608	528,795

R. (p. 63.)

In Sir William Petty's "Political Anatomy of Ireland," published in "Tracts chiefly relating to Ireland" (Dublin, 1769), that early authority writes (p. 356):—

"And now I shall digress again to consider, whether it were better for the commonwealth to restrain the expense of 150,000 optimates below £10 per annum each; or to beget a luxury in the 950,000 plebeians, so as to make them spend, and consequently earn, double what they at present do. To which I answer in brief, that the one shall increase the sordidness and squalor of living already too visible in 950,000 plebeians, with little benefit to the commonwealth; the other shall increase the splendour, art, and industry of the 950,000 to the great enriching of the commonwealth."

Messance deals with the problem far more energetically in the passage quoted in Appendix A. Here we find already an anticipation of the views of L. Brentano, "The Theory of Rises in Wages" in Hildebrand's "Jahrbücher für Nationalökonomie und Statistik," vol. 16, 1871, pp. 251–281; and of Heinrich Herkner, "Social Reform as a Condition of Economic Progress," Leipzig, 1891. In the latter essay the question of the text is dealt with *ex professo*.

S. (p. 67.)

In the volume for 1885 of the *Zeitschrift* of the Royal Saxon Statistical Bureau, District Inspector Von Schlieben published the results of his inquiries into the income and the food of the hand-loom weavers in the district of Zittau, which were made the foundation of a physiological investigation into the minimum required by a family for its subsistence. This last inquiry—"The Food of the Hand-loom Weavers in the district of Zittau"—by Dr. Carl von Rechenberg, was printed in 1890 (Leipzig, Hirzel), with the help of the Royal Saxon Academy of Sciences.

Rechenberg inquired into the condition of twenty-eight hand-loom weavers' families. Those of such families which had no children had an income of from £14 6s. to £23 18s. per year, an average of £19 15s.; those with children, an income of from £14 8s. to £65 7s. per year, an average of £28 8s. per year. This income was by no means exclusively derived from wages. On the contrary, in the calculations of the average, the letting value of the rooms not occupied by the householding families is reckoned in. The week's earnings of a hand-loom weaver working from fourteen to sixteen hours a day in winter, and from thirteen to fifteen in summer, varies from three to seven shillings, according to the sort of work he is engaged upon. To gain enough to cover the expenses of a family, the wife must also be a weaver. Moreover, when they are not at school the children are employed at winding.

Ninety per cent. of the food of these hand-loom weavers'

families consists of bread, potatoes, butter, and meal, of which
bread (55 per cent. of the entire energy-furnishing material)
forms the principle nutritive element, and potatoes almost
the only warm dish in the *menu.* The fare is almost entirely vegetarian, flesh-meat forming only ·7 per cent. of
the total food supply, while if herrings are included, the
proportion rises to 1·1 per cent., whereas, according to
Voit, a grown workman of average efficiency requires about
12 per cent of meat. The highest recorded consumption of
meat—one kilogramme a week per family—is found in the
case of two families only ; green vegetables are not much
eaten. The main beverage, which appears at all times of
the day, and almost at every meal, is coffee made of chicory,
roast barley or other coffee-substitutes. Brandy is not
drunk, and beer only now and then. The public-house is not
as a regular thing frequented.

The ordinary daily fare would be as follows :

Morning: coffee with milk, porridge, or bread and butter.

Mid-day : potatoes in their skins with salt and butter,
coffee and milk, bread.

Afternoon : coffee with milk, bread and butter.

Evening : skim or butter-milk, or new milk, bread and
butter, or potatoes with salt and butter, bread.

The consequence of this diet is that those who live on it
are underfed. It is true that they leave the mid-day meal
replete, and go to bed replete at night, but this feeling of
repletion is due to the preponderance of potatoes in their
food, which give that feeling, though they impart less nutri-
ment than the body needs for its adequate sustenance. The
families of the hand-loom weavers eat to repletion, and yet
eat too little.

The nourishment and general physical condition of such
families is therefore bad. The men look pale, and are as a
rule extremely thin ; the women in general are like the men.
Infants are nursed by the mother when possible for the first

four weeks at least. After they are weaned, the family diet, so unsuitable to children, makes them indeed full and round, but they are puffy, and as a rule have the so-called "potato-stomach." The older children, too, are pale and badly nourished as a rule. If their food were the same as is deemed necessary for ordinary well-fed children, hardly anything would be left of the family income for the nourishment of the grown-up members of the family.

The further consequence of this bad diet is great weakness. The people are incapable of any labour except that at the loom, which being done in a sitting position, employs, it is true, the arms and legs, but does not develop the muscles. Hence they are not capable of field labour during the ploughing and reaping season, and that despite the fact that the agricultural day-labourers in the Zittau district, and in general the poorer classes of the population who live much as the agricultural labourers do, though they are better nourished than the hand-loom weavers, are yet far from offering the type of a normal standard of nourishment and of a robust and efficient condition of body. But even as regards their own trade of weaving, they only do the easiest work. In the weaving of wide stuffs, in the case of which the abdomen suffers more from pressure on the beam of the loom, abdominal troubles set in,—sometimes slight, but sometimes of a severe and even mortal character, if the weaver does not give his stomach at least an hour's rest after the mid-day meal.

The work done for such pay in a thirteen to fifteen hours' day in summer, and a fourteen to sixteen hours' day in winter, is, according to Schlieben, as follows:

One piece of cotton of 61 metres length and ·77 metres width in eight days, daily piece-wage being 37 pfennig (Königshain).

Listado Checks, 41 metres long, ·66 metres wide, in five days, daily piece-wage 48 pfennig (Königshain).

I

Dish-cloths, 6 metres long, ·60 metres wide, in 6 days, daily piece-wage 57 pf.

Towelling, 34 metres long, ·42 metres wide, in 3½ days, daily piece-wage 57 pf.

Coloured Linens, 40 metres long, ·85 metres wide, in 9 days, daily piece-wage 55 pf.

Niederoderwitz and Mitteloderwitz.

Kreas Prints, 61 metres long, ·70 metres wide, in 9½ days, daily piece-wage 60 pf. Reichenau.

The essential cause of the thin, ill-nourished, inefficient physique of the hand-loom weavers is, according to Rechenberg, to be found in their inadequate food. What their diet needs above all is more meat (p. 59). But to carry out this proposal is practically impossible. Their diet has been so arranged that no improvement in the bill of fare is possible without increased expense. Even a larger consumption of bread and butter with the potatoes is impossible. If the nourishment of the family were to be transformed from an inadequate to an adequate one, and if the work of the man were to remain only moderate, the average income would have to be raised from £19 17s. to £22 5s., or 12 per cent. in the case of childless families, while in the case of families with children the average income would have to be raised from £28 6s. to £35 2s., or 22 per cent.; and lastly, were the work of the man to become severe, as it is on the land or in a factory, an additional £1 9s. yearly must, according to Rechenberg, be added.

In this connexion let no one imagine that the above data and calculations proceed from a man with a socialistic or even merely an over-sentimental bias. Dr. von Rechenberg begins the brief summary of the results of his inquiry with the words: "The hand-loom weavers of the Zittau district are an admirable instance how cheaply in case of extreme necessity subsistence can be had without injury to health, and a household kept going without any striking destitution." With the maintenance accessible to and the work furnished

by the German hand-loom weaver let us now compare the
budgets of English weavers, as stated by Schulze-Gävernitz
in his " Grossbetrieb," p. 233. Expenditure of a weaver-
family in Bacup, consisting of husband, wife, and seven
children :—total income £227, of which the father earns £45,
and the children £168; comparatively luxurious standard of
living, as may be seen in detail in Schulze-Gävernitz' pages,
total expenditure £172 10s. 10d., savings £55. Expenditure
of a weaver family in Darwen, consisting of husband, wife,
and three children between the ages of seven and eleven :
income, £101 7s.; expenditure £94 15s. 6d.; savings, £6.

T. (p. 24.)

MACAULAY'S SPEECH ON THE TEN HOURS BILL.

Delivered in the House of Commons on the
22nd of May, 1846.

[On the 29th of April, 1846, Mr. Fielden, Member for Oldham,
moved the second reading of a Bill for limiting the labour of young
persons in factories to ten hours a day. The debate was adjourned,
and was repeatedly resumed at long intervals. At length, on the
22nd of May, the Bill was rejected by 203 votes to 193.[1] On that
day the following speech was made.]

IT is impossible, Sir, that I can remain silent after the
appeal which has been made to me in so pointed a manner
by my honourable friend, the Member for Sheffield,[2] and even
if that appeal had not been made to me, I should have been
very desirous to have an opportunity of explaining the
grounds on which I shall vote for the second reading of this
bill.

It is, I hope, unnecessary for me to assure my honourable
friend that I utterly disapprove of those aspersions which

---

[1] It did not become law till June 8th, 1847.
[2] Mr. Ward.

have, both in this House and out of it, been thrown on the owners of factories. For that valuable class of men I have no feeling but respect and good will. I am convinced that with their interests the interests of the whole community, and especially of the labouring classes, are inseparably bound up. I can also with perfect sincerity declare that the vote which I shall give to-night will not be a factious vote. In no circumstances indeed should I think that the laws of political hostility warranted me in treating this question as a party question. But at the present moment I would much rather strengthen than weaken the hands of the Her Majesty's Ministers. It is by no means pleasant to me to be under the necessity of opposing them. I assure them, I assure my friends on this side of the House with whom I am so unfortunate as to differ, and especially my honourable friend the Member for Sheffield, who spoke, I must say, in rather too plaintive a tone, that I have no desire to obtain credit for humanity at their expense. I fully believe that their feeling towards the labouring people is quite as kind as mine. There is no difference between us as to ends: there is an honest difference of opinion as to means: and we surely ought to be able to discuss the points on which we differ without one angry emotion or one acrimonious word.

The details of the bill, Sir, will be more conveniently and more regularly discussed when we consider it in Committee. Our business at present is with the principle: and the principle, we are told by many gentlemen of great authority, is unsound. In their opinion, neither this bill, nor any other bill regulating the hours of labour, can be defended. This, they say, is one of those matters about which we ought not to legislate at all; one of those matters which settle themselves far better than any government can settle them. Now it is most important that this point should be fully cleared up. We certainly ought not to usurp functions which do not properly belong to us: but, on the other hand, we ought not to abdicate functions which do properly belong to us. I hardly know which is the greater pest to society, a paternal government, that is to say a prying, meddlesome government, which intrudes itself into every part of human life, and which thinks it can do everything for everybody better than anybody can do anything for himself; or a careless, lounging Government, which suffers grievances, such as it could at once remove, to grow and multiply, and which to all complaint and remonstrance has only one answer : " We must let things alone : we must let things take their course : we must let things find their level." There is no more important problem in politics than to ascertain the just mean between these two most pernicious extremes, to draw correctly the line which divides those cases in which it is the duty of the State to interfere from those cases in which it is the duty of the State to abstain from interference. In old times the besetting sin of rulers was undoubtedly an inordinate disposition to meddle. The lawgiver was always telling people how to keep their shops, how to till their fields, how to educate their children, how many dishes to have on their tables, how much a yard to give for the cloth which made their coats. He was always trying to remedy some evil which did not properly fall within his province : and the consequence was that he increased the evils which he attempted to remedy. He was so much shocked by the distress inseparable from scarcity that he made statutes against forestalling and regrating, and so turned the scarcity into a famine. He was so much shocked by the cunning and hardheartedness of money-lenders that he made laws against usury ; and the consequence was that the borrower, who, if he had been left unprotected, would have got money at ten per cent., could hardly, when protected get it at fifteen per cent. Some eminent political philosophers of the last century exposed with great ability the folly of such legislation, and, by doing so, rendered a great service to mankind. There has been a reaction, a reaction which has doubtless produced much good, but which, like most reactions, has not been without evils and dangers. Our statesmen cannot now be accused of being busybodies. But I am afraid that there is, even in some of the ablest and most upright among them, a tendency to the opposite fault. I will give an instance of what I mean. Fifteen years ago it became evident that railroads would soon, in every part of the kingdom, supersede to a great extent the old highways. The tracing of the new routes which were to join all the chief cities, ports, and naval arsenals of the island was a matter of the highest national importance. But, unfortunately, those who should have acted for the nation, refused to interfere. Consequently, numerous questions which were really public, questions which concerned the public convenience, the public prosperity, the public security, were treated as private questions. That the whole society was interested in having a good system of internal communication seemed to be forgotten. The speculator who wanted a large dividend on his shares, the landowner who wanted a large price for his acres, obtained a full hearing. But nobody applied to be heard on behalf of the community. The effects of that great error we feel, and we shall not soon cease to feel. Unless I am greatly mistaken, we are in danger of committing to-night an error of the same kind. The honourable Member for Montrose,[1] and my honourable friend the Member for Sheffield, think that the question before us is merely a question between the old and the new theories of commerce. They cannot understand how any friend of free trade can wish the legislature to interfere between the capitalist and the labourer. They say, "You do not make a law to settle the price of gloves, or the texture of gloves, or the length of credit which the glover shall give. You leave it to him to determine whether he will charge high or

---

[1] Mr. Hume, the veteran of the Free Trade party.

low prices, whether he will use strong or flimsy materials, whether he will trust or insist on ready money. You acknowledge that these are matters which he ought to be left to settle with his customers, and that we ought not to interfere. It is possible that he may manage his shop ill. But it is certain that we shall manage it ill. On the same grounds on which you leave the seller of gloves and the buyer of gloves to make their own contract, you ought to leave the seller of labour and the buyer of labour to make their own contract."

I have a great respect, Sir, for those who reason thus: but I cannot see this matter in the light in which it appears to them; and, though I may distrust my own judgment, I must be guided by it. I am, I believe, as strongly attached as any Member of this House to the principle of free trade, rightly understood. Trade, considered merely as trade, considered merely with reference to the pecuniary interest of the contracting parties, can hardly be too free. But there is a great deal of trade which cannot be considered merely as trade, and which affects higher than pecuniary interests. And to say that Government never ought to regulate such trade is a monstrous proposition, a proposition at which Adam Smith would have stood aghast. We impose some restrictions on trade for purposes of police. Thus, we do not suffer everybody who has a cab and a horse to ply for passengers in the streets of London. We do not leave the fare to be determined by the supply and the demand. We do not permit a driver to extort a guinea for going half a mile on a rainy day when there is no other vehicle on the stand. We impose some restrictions on trade for the sake of revenue. Thus, we forbid a farmer to cultivate tobacco on his own grounds. We impose some restrictions on trade for the sake of national defence. Thus, we compel a man who would rather be ploughing or weaving to go into the militia; and we fix the amount of pay which he shall receive without asking his consent. Nor is there in all this anything inconsistent with the soundest political economy. For the science of political economy teaches us only that we ought not, on commercial grounds, to interfere with the liberty of commerce; and we, in the cases which I have put, interfere with the liberty of commerce on higher than commercial grounds.

But now, Sir, to come closer to the case with which we have to deal, I say, first, that where the health of the community is concerned, it may be the duty of the State to interfere with the contracts of individuals; and to this proposition I am quite sure that Her Majesty's Government will cordially assent. I have just read a very interesting report signed by two members of that Government, the Duke of Buccleuch, and the noble earl who was lately Chief Commissioner of the Woods and Forests, and who is now Secretary for Ireland;[1] and since that report was laid before the House the noble earl himself has, with the sanction of the Cabinet, brought in a Bill for the protection of the Public Health. By this bill it is provided that no man shall be permitted to build a house upon his own land in any great town without giving notice to certain Commissioners. No man is to sink a cellar without the consent of these Commissioners. The house must not be of less than a prescribed width. No new house must be built without a drain. If an old house has no drain, the Commissioners may order the owner to make a drain. If he refuses they make a drain for him, and send him in the bill. They may order him to whitewash his house. If he refuses they may send people with pails and brushes to whitewash it for him, at his charge. Now, suppose that some proprietor of houses at Leeds or Manchester were to expostulate with the Government in the language in which the Government has expostulated with the supporters of this bill for the regula-

---

[1] The Earl of Lincoln.

tion of factories. Suppose he were to say to the noble earl. "Your lordship professes to be a friend to free trade. Your lordship's doctrine is that everybody ought to be at liberty to buy cheap, and sell dear. Why then may I not run up a house as cheap as I can, and let my rooms as dear as I can. Your lordship does not like houses without drains. Do not take one of mine then. You think my bedrooms filthy. Nobody forces you to sleep in them. Use your own liberty : but do not restrain that of your neighbours. I can find many a family willing to pay a shilling a week for leave to sleep in what you call a hovel. And why am I not to take the shilling which they are willing to give me ? And why are not they to have such shelter as, for that shilling, I can afford them ? Why did you send a man without my consent to clean my house, and then force me to pay for what I never ordered ? My tenants thought the house clean enough for them, or they would not have been my tenants; and if they and I were satisfied, why did you, in direct defiance of all the the principles of free trade, interfere between us ! "

This reasoning, Sir, is exactly of a piece with the reasoning of the honourable Member for Montrose, and of my honourable friend, the Member for Sheffield. If the noble earl will allow me to make a defence for him, I believe that he would answer to the objection thus : "I hold," he would say, " the sound doctrine of free trade. But your doctrine of free trade is an exaggeration, a caricature of the sound doctrine ; and by exhibiting such a caricature you bring discredit on the sound doctrine. We should have nothing to do with the contracts between you and your tenants, if those contracts affected only pecuniary interests. But higher than pecuniary interests is at stake. It concerns the commonwealth that the great body of the people should not live in a way which makes life wretched and short, which enfeebles the body and pollutes the mind. If, by living in houses which resemble hogstyes, great numbers of our countrymen have contracted the tastes of hogs, if they have become so familiar with filth and stench and contagion, that they burrow without reluctance in holes which would turn the stomach of any man of cleanly habits, that is only an additional proof that we have too long neglected our duties, and an additional reason for our now performing them."

Secondly, I say that where the public morality is concerned it may be the duty of the State to interfere with the contracts of individuals. Take the traffic in licentious books and pictures. Will anybody deny that the State may, with propriety, interdict that traffic? Or take the case of lotteries. I have, we will suppose an estate for which I wish to get twenty thousand pounds. I announce my intention to issue a thousand tickets at twenty pounds each. The holder of the number which is first drawn is to have the estate. But the magistrate interferes; the contract between me and the purchasers of my tickets is annulled; and I am forced to pay a heavy penalty for having made such a contract. I appeal to the principle of free trade, as expounded by the honourable gentlemen the Members for Montrose and Sheffield. I say to you, the legislators who have restricted my liberty, " What business have you to interfere between a buyer and a seller? If you think the speculation a bad one, do not take tickets. But do not interdict other people from judging for themselves." Surely you would answer, " You would be right if this were a mere question of trade; but it is a question of morality. We prohibit you from disposing of your property in this particular mode, because it is a mode which tends to encourage a most pernicious habit of mind, a habit of mind incompatible with all the qualities on which the well-being of individuals and of nations depends."

It must then, I think, be admitted that, where health is concerned, and where morality is concerned, the State is justified in interfering with the contracts of individuals.

And if this be admitted, it follows that the case with which we now have to do is a case for interference.

Will it be denied that the health of a large part of the rising generation may be seriously affected by the contracts which this bill is intended to regulate? Can any man who has read the evidence which is before us, can any man who has ever observed young people, can any man who remembers his own sensations when he was young, doubt that twelve hours a day of labour in a factory is too much for a lad of thirteen?

Or will it be denied that this is a question in which public morality is concerned? Can any one doubt,—none, I am sure, of my friends around me doubts,—that education is a matter of the highest importance to the virtue and happiness of a people? Now we know that there can be no education, without leisure, It is evident that, after deducting from the day twelve hours for labour in a factory, and the additional hours necessary for exercise, refreshment and repose, there will not remain time enough for education.

I have now, I think, shown that this bill is not in principle objectionable; and yet I have not touched the strongest part of our case. I hold that, where public health is concerned, and where public morality is concerned, the State may be justified in regulating even the contracts of adults. But we propose to regulate only the contracts of infants. Now, was there ever a civilised society in which the contracts of infants were not under some regulation? Is there a single member of this House who will say that a wealthy minor of thirteen ought to be at perfect liberty to execute a conveyance of his estate, or to give a bond for fifty thousand pounds? If anybody were so absurd as to say, "What has the Legislature to do with the matter? Why cannot you leave trade free? Why do you pretend to understand the boy's interest better than he understands it?" You will answer; "When he grows up he may squander his fortune away if he likes;

but at present the State is his guardian, and he shall not ruin himself till he is old enough to know what he is about." The minors whom we wish to protect have not indeed large property to throw away; but they are not the less our wards. Their only inheritance, the only fund to which they must look for their subsistence through life, is the sound mind in the sound body. And is it not our duty to prevent them from wasting that most precious wealth before they know its value."

But, it is said, this bill though it directly limits only the labour of infants will, by an indirect operation, limit also the labour of adults. Now, Sir, though I am not prepared to vote for a bill directly limiting the labour of adults, I will plainly say that I do not think that the limitation of the labour of adults would necessarily produce all those frightful consequences which which we have heard predicted. You cheer me in very triumphant tones, as if I had uttered some monstrous paradox. Pray does it not occur to any of you that the labour of adults is now limited in this country? Are you not aware that you are living in a society in which the labour of adults is limited to six days in seven? It is you, not I, who maintain a paradox opposed to the opinions and practices of all nations and ages. Did you ever hear of a single civilised state since the beginning of the world in which a certain portion of time was not set apart for the rest and recreation of adults by public authority? In general this arrangement has been sanctioned by religion. The Egyptians, the Jews, the Greeks, the Romans had their holidays; the Hindoo has his holidays; the Mussulman has his holidays; there are holidays in the Greek Church, holidays in the Church of Rome, holidays in the Church of England. Is it not amusing to hear a gentleman pronounce with confidence that any legislation which limits the labour of adults must produce consequences fatal to society, without once reflecting that in the society in which he lives and in every other society

that exists, or ever has existed, there has been such legislation
without any evil consequence? It is true that a Puritan
Government in England, and an Atheistical Government in
France, abolished the old holidays as superstitious. But those
Governments felt it to be absolutely necessary to institute new
holidays. Civil festivals were substituted for religious festivals. You will find among the ordinances of the Long Parliament a law providing that in exchange for the days of rest and
amusement, which the people had been used to enjoy at Easter,
Whitsuntide and Christmas, the second Tuesday in every
month should be given to the working man, and that any ap-
prentice who was forced to work on the second Tuesday of any
month might have his master up before a magistrate. The
French Jacobites decreed that the Sunday should no longer be
a day of rest; but they instituted another day of rest, the
Decade. They swept away the holidays of the Roman Catholic
Church; but they instituted another set of holidays, the
Sansculottides, one sacred to genius, one to industry, one to
opinion, and so on. I say, therefore, that the practice of
limiting by law the time of the labour of adults is so far from
being as some gentlemen seem to think, an unheard of and
monstrous practice, that it is a practice as universal as cook-
ery, as the wearing of clothes, as the use of domestic animals.

And has this practice been proved by experience to be pernicious? Let us take the instance with which we are most
familiar. Let us inquire what has been the effect of those
laws which, in our own country, limit the labour of adults to
six days in every seven. It is quite unnecessary to discuss
the question whether Christians be or be not bound by a
divine command to observe the Sunday. For it is evident
that, whether our weekly holiday be of divine or of human
institution, the effect on the temporal interests of Society
will be exactly the same. Now, is there a single argument
in the whole speech of my honourable friend the Member for
Sheffield which does not tell just as strongly against the laws

which enjoin the observance of the Sunday as against the bill on our table? Surely, if his reasoning is good for hours, it must be equally good for days.

He says, " If this limitation be good for the working people, rely on it that they will find it out, and that they will themselves establish it without any law." Why not reason in the same way about the Sunday? Why not say, " If it be a good thing for the people of London to shut their shops one day in seven, they will find it out, and will shut their shops without a law?" Sir, the answer is obvious. I have no doubt that, if you were to poll the shopkeepers of London, you would find an immense majority, probably a hundred to one, in favour of closing shops on the Sunday; and yet it is absolutely necessary to give to the wish of the majority the sanction of a law; for, if there were no such law, the minority, by opening their shops, would soon force the majority to do the same.

But, says my honourable friend, you cannot limit the labour of adults unless you fix wages. This proposition he lays down repeatedly, assures us that it is incontrovertible, and indeed seems to think it self-evident; for he has not taken the trouble to prove it. Sir, my answer shall be very short. We have, during many centuries, limited the labour of adults to six days in seven; and yet we have not fixed the rate of wages.

But, it is said, you cannot legislate for all trades; and therefore you had better not legislate for any. Look at the poor sempstress. She works far longer and harder than the factory child. She sometimes plies her needle fifteen, sixteen hours in the twenty-four. See how the housemaid works, up at six every morning, and toiling upstairs and down stairs till near midnight. You own that you cannot do anything for the sempstress and the housemaid.[1] Why then trouble

---

[1] By the legislation of 1867 the protection given to children working in factories was extended to sempstresses in workshops.

yourself about the factory child? Take care that by protecting one class you do not aggravate the hardships endured by the classes which you cannot protect. Why, Sir, might not all this be said, word for word, against the laws which enjoin the observance of the Sunday? There are classes of people whom you cannot prevent from working on the Sunday. There are classes of people whom, if you could, you ought not to prevent from working on the Sunday. Take the sempstress, of whom so much has been said. You cannot keep her from sewing and hemming all Sunday in her garret. But you do not think that a reason for suffering Covent Garden Market, and Leadenhall Market, and Smithfield Market, and all the shops from Mile End to Hyde Park to be open all Sunday. Nay, these factories about which we are debating—does anybody propose that they shall be allowed to work all Sunday? See, then, how inconsistent you are. You think it unjust to limit the labour of the factory child to ten hours a day, because you cannot limit the labour of the sempstress. And yet you see no injustice in limiting the labour of the factory child, aye, and of the factory man, to six days in the week, though you cannot limit the labour of the sempstress.

But, you say, by protecting one class we shall aggravate the sufferings of all the classes which we cannot protect. You say this; but you do not prove it; and all experience proves the contrary. We interfere on the Sunday to close the shops. We do not interfere with the labour of the housemaid. But are the housemaids of London more severely worked on the Sunday than on other days? The fact notoriously is the reverse. For your legislation keeps the public feeling in a right state, and thus protects indirectly those whom it cannot protect directly.

Will my honourable friend, the Member for Sheffield maintain that the law which limits the number of working days has been injurious to the working population? I am certain that he will not. How then can he expect me to believe that a law which limits the number of working hours must necessarily be injurious to the working population? Yet he, and those who agree with him, seem to wonder at our dulness because we do not at once admit the truth of the doctrine which they propound on this subject. They reason thus. We cannot reduce the number of hours of labour in factories without reducing the amount of production. We cannot reduce the amount of production without reducing the remuneration of the labourer. Meanwhile, foreigners, who are at liberty to work till they drop down dead at their looms, will soon beat us out of all the markets of the world. Wages will go down fast. The condition of our working people will be far worse than it is; and our unwise interference will, like the unwise interference of our ancestors with the dealings of the corn factor and the money lender, increase the distress of the very class which we wish to relieve.

Now, Sir, I fully admit that there might be such a limitation of the hours of labour as would produce the evil consequences with which we are threatened; and this, no doubt, is a very good reason for legislating with great caution, for feeling our way, for looking well to all the details of this bill. But it is certainly not true that every limitation of the hours of labour must produce these consequences. And I am, I must say surprised when I hear men of eminent ability and knowledge lay down the proposition that a diminution of the time of labour must be followed by a diminution of the wages of labour as a proposition universally true, as a proposition capable of being strictly demonstrated, as a proposition about which there can be no more doubt than about any theorem in Euclid. Sir, I deny the truth of the proposition; and for this plain reason. We have already, by law, greatly reduced the time of labour in factories. Thirty years ago, the late Sir Robert Peel[1] told the House that it was a common practice to make

---

[1] The father of the celebrated statesman.

children of eight years of age toil in mills fifteen hours a day,
A law has since been made which prohibits persons under
eighteen years of age from working in mills more than twelve
hours a day. That law was opposed on exactly the same
grounds on which the bill before us is opposed. Parliament
was told then, as it is told now, that with the time of labour
the quantity of production would decrease, that with the
quantity of production the wages would decrease, that our
manufacturers would be unable to contend with foreign
manufacturers, and that the condition of the labouring population instead of being made better by the interference of the
Legislature would be made worse. Read over those debates.
and you may imagine that you are reading the debate of this
evening. Parliament disregarded these prophecies. The
time of labour was limited. Have wages fallen? Has the
cotton trade left Manchester for France or Germany? Has
the condition of the working people become more miserable?
Is it not universally acknowledged that the evils which were
so confidently predicted have not come to pass? Let me be
understood. I am not arguing that, because a law which reduced the hours of daily labour from fifteen to twelve did not
reduce wages, a law reducing those hours from twelve to ten
or eleven cannot possibly reduce wages. That would be very
inconclusive reasoning. What I say is this, that since a law
which reduced the hours of daily labour from fifteen to twelve
has not reduced wages, the proposition that every reduction
of the hours of labour must necessarily reduce wages is a
false proposition. There is evidently some flaw in that demonstration which my honourable friend thinks so complete;
and what the flaw is we may perhaps discover if we look at
the analogous case to which I have so often referred.

Sir, exactly three hundred years ago great religious changes
were taking place in England. Much was said and written,
in that inquiring and innovating age, about the question
whether Christians were under a religious obligation to rest

K

from labour on one day in the week, and it is well known that the chief reformers, both here and on the Continent, denied the existence of any such obligation. Suppose then, that, in 1546, Parliament had made a law that there thould henceforth be no distinction between the Sunday and any other day. Now, Sir, our opponents, if they are consistent with themselves, must hold that such a law would have immensely increased the wealth of the country and the remuneration of the working man. What an effect, if their principles be sound, must have been produced by the addition of one-sixth to the time of labour! What an increase of production! What a rise of wages! How utterly unable must the foreign artisan, who still had his days of festivity and of repose, have found himself to maintain a competition with a people whose shops were open, whose markets were crowded, whose spades, and axes, and planes, and hods, and anvils, and looms were at work from morning till night on 365 days a year?

The Sundays of 300 years make up fifty years of our working days. We know what the industry of fifty years can do. We know what marvels the industry of the last fifty years has wrought. The arguments of my honourable friend irresistibly lead us to this conclusion, that if, during the last three centuries, the Sunday had not been observed as a day of rest, we should have been a far richer, a far more highly civilized people than we are now, and that the labouring classes especially would have been far better off than at present. But does he, does any Member of the House, seriously believe that this would have been the case? For my own part I have not the smallest doubt, that if we and our ancestors had, during the last three centuries, worked just as hard on the Sunday as on the week days, we should have been at this moment a poorer people and a less civilized people than we are; that there would have been less production than there has been, that the wages of the labourer would have been lower than they are, and that some other nation would have been now making cotton stuffs and cutlery for the whole world.

Of course, Sir, I do not mean to say that a man will not produce more in a week by working seven days than by working six days. But I very much doubt whether at the end of a year he will generally have produced more by working seven days a week than by working six days a week; and I firmly believe that, at the end of twenty years, he will have produced much less by working seven days a week than by working six days a week. In the same manner I do not deny that a factory child will produce more in a single day, by working twelve hours than by working ten hours, and by working fifteen hours than by working twelve hours. But I do deny that a great society in which children work fifteen or even twelve hours a day will, in the lifetime of a generation, produce as much as if those children had worked less. If we consider man merely in a commercial point of view, if we consider him merely as a machine for the production of worsted and calico, let us not forget what a piece of mechanism he is, how fearfully and wonderfully made. We do not treat a fine horse or a sagacious dog exactly as we treat a spinning jenny. Nor will any slaveholder, who has sense enough to know his own interest, treat his human chattels exactly as he treats his horses and his dogs. And would you treat the free labourer of England like a mere wheel or pulley? Rely on it that intense labour, beginning too early in life, continued too long every day, stunting the growth of the body, stunting the growth of the mind, leaving no time for healthful exercise, leaving no time for intellectual culture, must impair all those high qualities which have made our country great. Your overworked boys will become a feeble and ignoble race of men, the parents of a more feeble and more ignoble progeny; nor will it be long before the deterioration of the labourer will injuriously affect those very interests to which his physical and moral energies have been sacrificed. On the other hand, a day of rest recurring in every week, two or three hours of leisure, exercise, innocent amusement or useful study, recurring every day, must improve the whole man, physically, morally, intellectually; and the improvement of the man will improve all that the man produces. Why is it, Sir, that the Hindoo cotton manufacturer, close to whose door the cotton grows, cannot, in the bazaar of his own town, maintain a competition with the English cotton manufacturer, who has to send thousands of miles for the raw material, and who has then to send the wrought material thousands of miles to market? You will say that it is owing to the excellence of our machinery. And to what is the excellence of our machinery owing? How many of the improvements which have been made in our machinery do we owe to the ingenuity and patient thought of working men? Adam Smith tells us in the first chapter of his great work, that you can hardly go to a factory without seeing some very pretty machine,—that is his expression,—devised by some labouring man. Hargreaves, the inventor of the spinning jenny, was a common artisan. Crompton, the inventor of the mule jenny, was a working man. How many hours of the labour of children would do so much for our manufactures as one of these improvements has done? And in what sort of society are such improvements most likely to be made? Surely in a society in which the faculties of the working people are developed by education. How long will you wait before any negro, working under the lash in Louisiana, will contrive a better machinery for squeezing the sugar canes? My honourable friend seems to me, in all his reasonings about the commercial prosperity of nations, to overlook entirely the chief cause on which that prosperity depends. What is it, sir, that makes the great difference between country and country? Not the exuberance of soil;

not the mildness of climate; not mines, nor havens, nor
rivers. These things are indeed valuable when put to their
proper use by human intelligence; but human intelligence
can do much without them; and they without human intelligence can do nothing. They exist in the highest degree in
regions of which the inhabitants are few, and squalid, and
barbarous, and naked, and starving; while on sterile rocks,
amidst unwholesome marshes, and under inclement skies,
may be found immense populations, well fed, well lodged,
well clad, well governed. Nature meant Egypt and Sicily
to be the gardens of the world. They once were so. Is it
anything in the earth or in the air that makes Scotland more
prosperous than Egypt, that makes Holland more prosperous
than Sicily? No; it was the Scotchman that made Scotland;
it was the Dutchman that made Holland. Look at North
America. Two centuries ago the sites on which now arise
mills and hotels, and banks, and colleges, and churches, and
the Senate Houses of flourishing commonwealths, were
deserts abandoned to the panther and the bear. What has
made the change? was it the rich mould, or the redundant
rivers? No; the prairies were as fertile, the Ohio and the
Hudson were as broad and as full then as now. Was the
improvement the effect of some great transfer of capital from
the old world to the new? No; the emigrants generally
carried out with them no more than a pittance; but they
carried out the English heart and head and arm; and the
English heart and head and arm turned the wilderness into
cornfield and orchard, and the huge trees of the primeval
forest into cities and fleets. Man, man is the great instru-
ment that produces wealth. The natural difference between
Campania and Spitzbergen is trifling, when compared with
the difference between a country inhabited by men full of
bodily and mental vigour, and a country inhabited by men
sunk in bodily and mental decrepitude. Therefore it is that
we are not poorer but richer, because we have, through

many ages, rested from our labour one day in seven. That day is not lost. While industry is suspended, while the plough lies in the furrow, while the exchange is silent, while no smoke ascends from the factory, a process is going on quite as important to the wealth of nations, as any process which is performed on more busy days. Man, the machine of machines, the machine compared with which all the contrivances of the Watts and the Arkwrights are worthless, is repairing and winding up, so that he returns to his labours on the Monday with clearer intellect, with livelier spirits, with renewed corporal vigour. Never will I believe that what makes a population stronger, and healthier, and wiser, and better, can ultimately make it poorer. You try to frighten us by telling us, that in some German factories, the young work seventeen hours in the twenty-four, that they work so hard that among thousands there is not one who grows to such a stature that he can be admitted into the army;[1] and you ask whether, if we pass this bill we can possibly hold our own against such competition as this? Sir, I laugh at the thought of such competition. If ever we are forced to yield the foremost place among commercial nations, we shall yield it not to a race of degenerate dwarfs, but to some people pre-eminently vigorous in body and in mind.

For these reasons, Sir, I approve of the principle of this bill, and shall, without hesitation, vote for the second reading. To what extent we ought to reduce the hours of labour, is a question of more difficulty. I think that we are in the situation of a physician who has satisfied himself that there is a disease, and that there is a specific remedy for the

---

[1] An allusion to the report of Lieut.-General von Horn to Frederick William III., to the effect that the factory districts no longer supplied their full contingent of recruits to the army. Cf. Anton, "Geschichte der Preussischen Gesetzgebung," p. 82 (Leipsic, 1891).

disease, but who is not certain what quantity of that medicine the patient's constitution will bear. Such a physician would probably administer his remedy by small doses, and carefully watch its operation. I cannot help thinking that, by at once reducing the hours of labour from twelve to ten, we should hazard too much. The change is great and ought to be cautiously and gradually made. Suppose that there should be an immediate fall of wages, which is not impossible. Might there not be a violent reaction? Might not the public take up a notion that our legislation had been erroneous in principle, though in truth our error would have been an error, not of principle, but but merely of degree? Might not Parliament be induced to retrace its steps? Might we not find it difficult to maintain even the present limitation? The wisest course would, in my opinion, be to reduce the hours of labour from twelve to eleven,[1] to observe the effect of that experiment, and if, as I hope and believe, the result should be satisfactory, then to make a further reduction from eleven to ten. This is a question, however, which will be with more advantage considered when we are in Committee.

One word, Sir, before I sit down, in answer to my noble friend[2] near me. He seems to think that this bill is ill-timed. I own that I cannot agree with him. We carried up on Monday last to the bar of the Lords a bill[3] which will remove the most hateful and pernicious restriction that ever was laid on trade. Nothing can be more proper than to apply, in the same week, a remedy to a great evil of a directly opposite kind.

---

[1] By the Act of June 8th, 1847, the hours of labour were reduced from twelve to ten, and the reduction did not prove too abrupt, as Macaulay feared it might.

[2] Lord Morpeth.

[3] The Bill repealing the Corn Laws.

As lawgivers, we have two great faults to confess and to repair. We have done that which we ought not to have done; we have left undone that which we ought to have done. We have regulated that which we should have left to regulate itself; we have left unregulated that which we were bound to regulate. We have given to some branches of industry a protection which has proved their bane; we have withheld from public health and public morals, the protection which was their due. We have prevented the labourer from buying his loaf where he could get it cheapest; but we have not prevented him from ruining his body and mind by premature and immoderate toil. I hope that we have seen the last, both of a vicious system of interference and of a vicious system of non-interference, and that our poorer countrymen will no longer have reason to attribute their sufferings either to our meddling or to our neglect.

INDEX.

Achenbach, Prussian Minister of Trade, maintains that high wages are equivalent to low production, 10; misunderstands the facts on which he relies, 12.

Agriculture in Australia, effect of high wages on, 54.

Allan, Sunderland shipbuilder, on short hours, 36.

America, superior efficiency of labour in, 52.

Anderson maintains that low pay is not equivalent to cheap work, 6.

Atkinson, Edward, quoted, 34.

Beaufoy, M.P., Mr., on economy of time due to eight hours day, 58.

Bell, Sir Lowthian, his view of wages and production criticised, 15; his statement about the Iron Trade, 92–99.

Brassey, his testimony that high wages are equivalent to high production, 9, 10; his comparison of English with Russian workman, 38.

Bright, John, his outburst against Ten Hours Bill, 23.

Camphausen, Prussian Finance Minister, maintains that high pay is equivalent to low production, 10.

Chamberlain advocates Eight Hours Day, 37, 106.

Chevalier, Michel, 8.

Child maintains that high wages are equivalent to low production, 2, 3.

Coal, increased output of, between 1854 and 1889, 35; effect of shorter hours in English and German mines, 11, 35; technical improvements in mining, 54, 55.

137

Concordia, weekly periodical on the Labour Question, 11, 88.

Cotton Trade, in Lancashire, 25, 59–62, 103, 104, 109, 110; in Germany, 63–67.

Cox, Harold, on Eight Hours Day, 105.

Crowe, Sir Joseph, his fallacious comparison of English and German labour, 15, 89.

Dickens quoted, with reference to the hostility of manufacturers to factory legislation, 25.

Dollfus, effect of short hours in works of, 35.

Durham, Colliers' working day in, 22.

" *Edinburgh Review* " referred to, 27, 102.

Eight Hours Day, economises time, 57, 58, 105, 106.

Elbœuf, Messance on woollen industry at, 5.

Engel, on English factory labour in the thirties and forties, 58.

Factories, technical progress in, 60–62.

Forster, on the relation of wages to production, 3.

Franklin maintains that low pay is not equivalent to cheap work, 6.

Frommel, his Augsberg workmen refuse to do more work for more wages, 45.

" *Hard Times*," quoted, 25.

Helm, Elijah, on English Cotton Industry, 103, 104; transference of cotton spinning from North to South Lancashire, 108, 109.

Hertzka, Theodor, his estimate of the average output of the Austrian miner, 13, 14.

Hofmann compares the woodchoppers of Berlin and Labiau, 8.

Holy Days, 21; at Meran, no benefit to the people, 39.

Houghton maintains that high wages are equivalent to low production, 2, 3.

Houldsworth, Sir W., his table of spinner's output, hours, and wages, 8.

Hours of Labour, shorter, demanded by workmen, 19; very long at beginning of machinery period, 21; steadily shortened during last seventy-five years, 22; Dickens quoted, 25; Bonamy

Price opposed to short, 28;
Ernest von Plener on, 29, 30;
tables showing increased
production resulting from
short hours, 30; her long
hours no advantage to India,
31; short hours have bene-
fited textile industry, 31;
workers with regularly
short, outstrip those with
regularly long, 33; in Massachusetts, 34; James Stephens'
testimony in favour of
short, 34; in mines, Professor
Munro on, 35; in Switzer-
land, 35; at Stuttgart, 36;
at Sunderland, 36; short,
cause of greater efficiency of
American workman, 33;
effect of short, in Northumberland and Westphalia,
49, 50; fallacy of assumption
that shorter will lead to absorption of unemployed, 68–
70; Mundella quoted on
disadvantages of long, 72.

India, her low wages and long
hours no advantage to her
trade, 31; comparison of
workman in, with the
English, 33.
Industry, Royal Commission
of Inquiry appointed in 1885

to inquire into causes of
depression in, 14; table
showing development of the
cotton from 1835 to 1890, 25;
cotton, increased by shorter
hours, 32; English cotton,
more prosperous than Ger-
man, 58; Irish cotton, and
its cheap labour, 59; Lancashire becomes centre of,
from its high wages, 59.
Iron, puddling of, replaced
by superior methods in
England, but retained in
Germany, 56, 57; Inquiry-
Commission in Germany,
99–101; its Report of 1879
compares English and Ger-
man workman to the advan-
tage of former, 16.

Johnson, Dr., quoted, 40.

Kärger, his "Sachsengangerei,"
41–43.

Labour, Justus Moser on extra labour done in off hours,
19; to increase the efficiency
of, improvements in the conditions of labour must be permanent, 47, 48; superior efficiency of, in America, 52, 53;
improved conditions of, in

coal-mining, leads to technical improvements, 54–56; increased division of, in English factories, 60; decrease of child-labour in factories, 61, 107.

Laissez-faire, English representatives of, 24.

Lancashire, its high-paid labour makes it centre of cotton trade, 59; transference of cotton-spinning from North to South of, 108, 109.

Laveleye, Emile de, on slowness of German workman compared with Belgian and French, 33.

Macaulay, Lord, speech on Ten Hours Bill, 115.

McCulloch endorses Adam Smith's view, 6.

Machinery, agitation in Lancashire against, 44; importance of cheap, 51; great perfection of in America, 52, 53; superiority of agricultural in Australia, due to high wages, 54; child-labour in factories eliminated by improvement in, 61.

Manchester Chamber of Commerce, its opinion on the superior cheapness of English, as compared with Indian cotton-spinning, 31.

Marshall, Professor, his defence of the classical political economy, 28.

Martin-process, 56, 57.

Martineau, Harriet, her deductive method adversely criticised, 27.

Massachusetts, evidence from, favourable to shorter hours and higher wages, 34.

Mather, William, his testimony in favour of short hours, 33; introduces eight hours day experimentally, 37.

Messance, quoted by Adam Smith as showing that the poor do more work in cheap than in dear years, 5, 79–87.

Migration, effect of on Russian peasants, 40; Kärger, his book on migratory labour in Saxony, 41; from Upper Silesia, 41; effect of, on Italian navvies, 42; of South Sea Islanders, 42, 43.

Mill, John Stuart, his wish to confine factory legislation to children, 27.

Moser, Justus, on labour done in off hours, 19, 20.

Mülhausen, imports cotton-goods for printing from Lancashire, 10; short hours in, 35.

Mundella quoted on disadvantages of long hours, 72.

Munro, Professor, on increased output in English Coal mines, 35, 54, 55.

Nasse, Erwin, Professor, justifies the miners' protest against Achenbach's Rescript, 11.

Northumberland, Colliers' working-day in, 22.

Peel, Sir Robert, quoted on Factory child labour, 21; quoted by Macaulay, 128.

Petty, Sir William, maintains that high wages are equivalent to low production, 2, 3, 110.

Plener, Ernest von, quoted on the evils of long hours, 31, 32.

Postlethwait on the relation of wages to production, 3.

Preston, effect of cotton spinners' strike at, in 1853, 59.

Price, Professor Bonamy, opposed to short hours, 28.

Roscher, compares the day-labourers of Mecklenburg

and Thuringia, 8; referred to, 48.

Rouen, Messance on linen and silk industry at, 5.

Saxony, migration thither of Silesian labourers, 41, 42.

Schlieben, District Inspector von, on conditions of life of handloom weavers in Zittau, 111–115.

Schoenhof, Jacob, his conclusion that low wages and long hours mean dear production, and *vice-versa*, 17, 18; quoted to show that short hours mean large production, 32; 33; quoted, 51; on superior efficiency of labour in America, 52; quoted to show that high wages mean cheap production, 74.

Schulze-Gavernitz, Gerhart v., 2; shows in his *Grossbetrieb* how English cotton industry has gone ahead in spite of higher wages and shorter hours, 17; his work on *Grossbetrieb*, 38; on Lancashire factory labour, 44, 45; compares English cotton industry with German, to the advantage of former, 58, 65–68.

Scott, John, shipbuilder, his evidence before the Royal Commission on the Depression of Trade and Industry, 104, 105.

Senior represents Adam Smith's view, 6; cites the evidence of English manufacturers in France, that lower wages mean higher price of labour and more costly production, 7; against shortening the working day, 24; his deductive method adversely criticised, 27; favours extension of factory legislation in the sixties, 28, 29; his speech at Social Science Congress, 101, 102.

Siemens, Werner von, his copper works in the Caucasus, 107, 108.

Smith, Adam, maintains that high wages are equivalent to large production, 3-5; his doctrine proved by the facts appealed to by Achenbach's Rescript, and by the report of the Liège Mining administration, 12; quoted by Macaulay, 132.

Stephens, James, his testmoiny in favour of short hours, 34.

Stuttgart, short hours tried in a factory at, 36.

Switzerland, short hours in, 35.

Temple maintains that high wages are equivalent to low production, 2.

Ten Hours Act, John Bright's speech on, 23; effect of, 58, 59, 102, 103; Lord Macaulay's speech on, 115 foll.

Trade Unions, the Depression of Trade Commission exonerates them from a share in causing the depression, 14.

Tucker, Josiah, maintains that high wages are equivalent to low production, 2, 3.

Vanderlint on the relation of wages to production, 3.

Unemployed, will not be " absorbed " by shortening the working day, 68-70.

Wages, advantage of high, asserted by Adam Smith, 4; McCulloch, 6; Senior, 7; Roscher, 8; Brassey, 9; Schoenhof, 17, 53; denied by Camphausen and Achenbach, 10; high, coincident with high output in coal-mining in Germany, 11 ; in province of Liège, 12 ; in Austria, 13 ; German Iron Inquiry Commission favourable to high, 16 ; high, combined with low labour-cost, in United States, 17, 53 ; in English cotton trade, 45 ; high, and intense labour, 45 ; high, develop mechanical invention, 51 ; low, facilitate the retention of obsolete and inferior processes, 57, 75.

Wallace, Mackenzie, on effect of migration on Russian peasants, 40.

Wallace, Robert, his " Rural Economy in Australia," 54.

Webb, Sidney, on Eight Hours Day, 105.

Westminster Review referred to, 27, 102.

Working Day, see *Hours.*

Young, Arthur, maintains that high wages are equivalent to low production, 2, 3 ; modifies his view in later writings, 6, 87.

Butler & Tanner. The Selwood Printing Works. Frome, and London.